*In Pursuit
of Maturity*

In Pursuit
of Maturity

J. OSWALD SANDERS

**Lamplighter
Books** Grand Rapids,
Michigan
Zondervan Publishing House

IN PURSUIT OF MATURITY

Lamplighter Books are published by the
Zondervan Publishing House
l4l5 Lake Drive, S.E., Grand Rapids, Michigan 49506

Library of Congress Cataloging in Publication Data

Sanders, J. Oswald (John Oswald), 1902–
In pursuit of maturity.

Includes bibliographies and indexes.
1. Christian life—1960– . I. Title.
BV4501.2.S178 1986   248.8'4   86-9139
ISBN 0-310-32511-0

Edited by David Hazard

Printed in the United States of America

88 89 90 91 92 93 94 / EP / 11 10 9 8 7 6 5 4 3

To my beloved niece
Peggy Adair
who has with meticulous care
typed the manuscripts of most
of my books

CONTENTS

PREFACE

The apostle Paul encapsulated the goal of his ministry in nine words: "That I may present every man mature in Christ" (Col. 1:28 RSV). It was to this end he devoted all his energies.

The need for this maturity is no less urgent in the space age, and it is the responsibility of every member of the body of Christ to "continue progressing towards maturity" (Heb. 6:1 WILLIAMS).

In our pursuit of maturity, we are not left to our own meager resources. We have not only the glowing example and pattern of that maturity in our Lord Himself but also the dynamic for its attainment in the powerful ministry of the Holy Spirit. As Paul puts it, "We . . . are being transformed into his likeness with ever-increasing glory, which comes from the Lord, who is the Spirit" (2 Cor. 3:18).

The maturity Paul has in view is not confined to the spiritual life alone, but will profoundly affect body, mind, and emotions as well. Our maturity is to be lived out in the context of the body.

It has been emphasized rightly that full Christian experience cannot be realized except in the context of a caring Christian community. In a day of excessive individualism, this aspect of the maturing process should not be ignored. Maturity cannot be fully realized apart from the grace of God and in the fellowship of His people.

This book has been written in the hope that it may encourage some to continue more ardently in their pursuit of Christian maturity.

J. Oswald Sanders

Auckland, New Zealand
1984

1

In Pursuit of Maturity

Let us go on to maturity. —Hebrews 6:1

Two pastors happened to be walking in opposite directions on the main street of their city. One was striding along at a great pace, and as he passed by, the other pastor inquired, "Where are you hurrying to?"

"I'm hurrying on to perfection," was the rejoinder.

"Well, if that's the case," said the other, "I had better not hinder you, for you have such a long, long journey ahead of you."

Most of us would concede the appropriateness of the jest to our own case, for are we not very conscious that we have a long road ahead of us as we strive to attain mature Christian character? The example of the perfect life of Christ seems so far removed from the level of our attainment that at times we grow discouraged. Nevertheless the exhortation of Hebrews 6:1 is addressed to all believers, and it carries within a note of optimism.

In his commentary of Hebrews 6:1, Bishop Westcott points out that there are three possible translations, each of which warns against a possible danger:

"Let us go on to maturity" suggests the possibility that (1) we may *stop too soon*, feeling that we have arrived. Paul contradicted this complacency when he wrote, "Not as though I had already attained, either were already perfect . . . I press toward the mark . . ." (Phil.

3:12, 14 KJV). (2) "Let us press on" suggests that we may succumb to *the peril of discouragement* and drop our bundle. No, we are to heed the warning and "continue progressing toward maturity," as the tense of the verb indicates. (3) "Let us be borne on," warns against the peril of *thinking that we are left to do it alone.* In the pursuit of maturity we have the fullest cooperation of the triune God. It takes all three of these possible translations to convey the wealth and significance of these few words.[1]

In a very honest and self-revealing manner, Lane Adams describes his pursuit of maturity:

> In this struggle after maturity I often sought the counsel of others by reading books and by veiled roundabout questioning of men I admired. Never admitting to the real specifics, I yet longed to know more about what brought maturity in the Christian life, because it was becoming obvious to me I didn't have it. (How hard it was for me to face and admit this to myself!)
>
> There was a general agreement on what brought maturity. Serious in-depth daily study of the Bible; a living relationship to God in prayer; regular sharing of your faith in Christ through witness; involvement in the local church and other service to mankind as opportunities presented themselves. All of this I had been doing for several years. Why were the results not greater?
>
> I received no help at all from others. Answers ranged anywhere from a conception of conversion that presupposed maturity arriving overnight, to an honest "I don't know."[2]

This poignant experience of a sincere seeker after maturity is not uncommon, and yet it need not be so. In the manifesto of His kingdom, our Lord gave this ringing assurance: "Blessed are those who hunger and thirst for righteousness, for they will be filled" (Matt. 5:6). An increasing spiritual maturity is an attainable goal, not a constantly receding mirage.

In Paul's exposition of the purpose he had in view in proclaiming Christ, he made it clear that his objective was more than evangelism: "We proclaim him, admonishing and teaching everyone with all wisdom, *so that we may present everyone perfect [mature] in Christ*" (Col. 1:28, italics mine). And he pursued his objective with intensity, for he added, "To this end I labor, struggling with all his energy, which so powerfully works in me" (Col. 1:29).

In another letter Paul further elucidated the standard of maturity that he held up before the Ephesian Christians. He prayed that they might *"reach unity in the faith and in the knowledge of the Son of God and become mature,* attaining to the whole measure of the fullness of Christ" (Eph. 4:13, italics mine). It was for this purpose Christ gave to His church the spiritually gifted men referred to in Ephesians 4:11–12.

Reaching for maturity is a dynamic process that continues as long as we live. The Christian life is not a hundred-meter dash, but a marathon that will test our spiritual stamina to the limit. There is no such thing as instant maturity or instant sainthood.

> *Let no one think that sudden in a minute*
> *All is accomplished and the work is done,*
> *Though in thine earliest dawn thou shouldst begin it,*
> *Scarce were it ended in thy setting sun.*
> F.W.H. Myers, "St. Paul"

Maturing is a slow process. It is achieved only with difficulty—physical, mental, and spiritual. It is a process that never ends, but it can be accelerated by obedience to the spiritual laws laid down in Scripture. This should save us from discouragement. As Henry Ward Beecher once said, "The Church is not a gallery for the exhibition of eminent Christians, but a school for the education of imperfect ones."

A Chinese proverb says: "If you are working for a year, plant rice. If you are working for a century, plant a tree. If you are working for eternity, plant a man."

When God is developing a life for eternity, He is in no hurry. A pumpkin will mature in three months, but an oak tree takes a century, and there are no shortcuts. This principle of growth is equally applicable in the spiritual realm. Clement of Rome so applied it many centuries ago:

> The process of growth in a tree is slow but inevitable. The foliage falls after the harvest, but then in the Spring a bud appears, and later flowers. These in turn lead on to young unripe grapes, and finally the full cluster. It does not take very long, it is true, but the whole process must take place. No stage can be left out. There are no shortcuts to a crop of good, mature fruit.
>
> Neither can God's purposes be hurried. No stage can be left out. The whole process must take place. But let us be in no doubt that His promises will be fulfilled.[3]

The principle of growth in spiritual maturity is often taught and illustrated in Scripture. Jesus drew a parallel with the wheat harvest: "First the stalk, then the head, then the full kernel in the head" (Mark 4:28). John recognized this principle in his first letter when he wrote, "I write to you, dear children . . . I write to you, fathers . . . I write to you, young men . . ." (1 John 2:12, 13).

In human life there are three stages of maturity. The first is *dependent childhood,* when the infant has to rely on others for almost everything. The child makes no decisions and needs constant care and nurture. The second stage of maturity is *independent adolescence,* when the developing child begins to realize self-hood and demands the right to make his or her own decisions. The child is no longer content to be dependent on others but feels competent to choose his own destiny. Finally the person moves into *maturing adulthood.* The person's powers are developed, and he or she is now a responsible person in his or her own right. The person has attained adult status and accepts full responsibility for his or her own life and actions.

A similar progression is seen in our growth in Christian maturity. The new life that enters at conversion is the infant life. "Like newborn babies, crave spiritual milk, so that by it you may grow up in your salvation" (1 Pet. 2:2). The embryo life in the new believer is fragile and requires loving care and nurture in the dependent stage. A nursing mother is needed as long as the child remains a milk-drinking infant. Gradually the child will progress to solid food as he or she moves on to adolescence.

Next comes the independent adolescent stage when the young believer has found his or her feet and becomes impatient of restraints. Spiritual adolescence, like physical adolescence, is sometimes a rather tempestuous period. The sanctity of old institutions and methods is challenged. The wisdom of age is questioned, and the young person steps out on his or her own. Provided it is kept within limits, this is a normal development, but the life must be brought under the Lordship of Christ and the control of the Holy Spirit if it is to attain full spiritual maturity.

The third stage is that of progressive maturity. Adulthood has been attained, but there is endless scope for growth. We are to grow up into Christ "in everything," every part of life finding its center and goal in Him.

Commenting on Paul's exhortation to "grow up into him who is the Head" (Eph. 4:15), Ronald Knox points out that a baby's head is very large in proportion to the rest of the body. But as the body develops, it grows up in correct proportion to the head. As the maturing believer grows to match the Head, he or she progressively moves toward the "measure of the stature of the fullness of Christ" (Eph. 4:13 KJV).[4]

There is to be no standing still in our pursuit of maturity. Oliver Cromwell inscribed in his Bible a pregnant motto: "He who ceases to be better, ceases to be good."

> *Let me then be always growing,*
> *Never standing still,*
> *Listening, learning, better knowing*
> *Thee and Thy blessed will.*
>
> Anonymous

The attaining of spiritual maturity takes time, but time alone is no guarantee of growth. As has been pointed out, maturity sometimes outruns time. Do we not sometimes remark of some child, "She is mature for her age"? Or of another, "Will he never grow up?" Maturity, whether physical or spiritual, does not always progress at a constant pace, and this is especially so in the adolescent stage. Maturity is the natural outworking of the growing process of the soul and is organic, not mechanical.

"It is not the time itself that produces the maturity," writes Charles C. Ryrie, "rather the progress made and the growth achieved are all-important. Rate multiplied by time equals distance, so that the distance to maturity may be covered in a shorter time if the rate of growth is accelerated; and it will be accelerated if none of the control which ought to be given to the Holy Spirit is retained by self."[5]

All growth is progressive, and the more complex and delicate the organism, the more time it will take to reach maturity. But it should be said that one is mature not merely after a certain lapse of time, but after the essential laws of spiritual growth have been obeyed. Physical growth is determined by observance of the laws of nutrition and health. Spiritual growth is spontaneous when the soul is fed consistently from the Word, when it breathes the pure air of prayer, and when it cultivates fellowship with the people of God. On the other hand, our growth can be stunted by failing to provide congenial spiritual conditions.

If we are to exercise an influential spiritual ministry, it will grow out of the soil of a faithfully observed devotional life.

> *Thank God! A man can grow!*
> *He is not bound*
> *With earthward gaze to creep along the*
> *ground:*
> *Though his beginning be but poor and low,*
> *Thank God, a man can grow!*
>
> C. Cowman

NOTES

1. As quoted in W. H. Griffith Thomas, *Let Us Go On* (Chicago: B.I.C.A.), p. 73.
2. Lane Adams, *How Come It's Taking Me So Long To Get Better?* (Wheaton, Illinois: Tyndale House Publishers, Inc., 1981), p. 19.
3. David Winter, *Faith Under Fire* (Wheaton, Illinois: Harold Shaw Publishers, 1983), p. 14.
4. Ronald Knox, *St. Paul's Gospel* (London, 1953), p. 84.
5. Charles C. Ryrie, *Balancing the Christian Life* (Chicago: Moody Press, 1969), p. 13.

2

What Constitutes
Christian Maturity?

We proclaim him, admonishing and teaching everyone with all wisdom, so that we may present everyone perfect in Christ. To this end I labor, struggling with all his energy, which so powerfully works in me.
—Colossians 1:28–29

Epaphras, who is one of you and a servant of Christ Jesus, sends greetings. He is always wrestling in prayer for you, that you may stand firm in all the will of God, mature and fully assured. —Colossians 4:12

It will help to clear the ground if we consider first several factors that do *not* constitute Christian maturity. A study of the relevant Scripture verses will reveal these facts.

First, *Christian maturity is not an aging process.* Gray hairs and spiritual maturity are not necessarily wedded. Because we are aging, we should not conclude that of necessity we are progressing in maturity. Gray hairs can cover a person whose reactions to people and circumstances are anything but mature. It has been said that it is the *intensity* of years and not their *extensity* that is a true measure of maturity, for maturity is an attitude of life. It is our attitudes, not our arteries, that determine the quality of our life. Our age is beyond our control, but whatever our age, our attitudes can be changed by the power of grace and a holy purpose.

Spiritual growth is not measured by the calendar, and it can continue to the hour of death or translation if we are willing to comply with the laws governing growth.

Spiritual maturity is not instantaneous and final. If it were so, what would be the point of the exhortation in Hebrews 6:1, "Let us go on to maturity," (or, catching the correct sense of the verb, "Let us continue progressing toward maturity")? The whole tenor of Scripture is against the idea that one supreme act of decision permanently secures to us all the blessings of sanctification.

No living thing comes to maturity instantaneously. In the attainment of intellectual maturity, there is no alternative to the student painfully working through the prescribed courses. Nor is it any different in the spiritual life. Growth toward spiritual maturity will of necessity involve moral effort, discipline, renunciation, and perseverance in pursuit of the goal. There are no shortcuts.

Spiritual maturity is not automatic as a result of the mastery of scriptural teachings. Of course that is an essential element in attaining maturity, but of itself it cannot produce maturity. The accumulation of biblical information is of immense value, but it is only as the principles of Scripture are worked out in daily obedience that spiritual growth is advanced. Bible study can be largely an intellectual exercise that leaves the life unchanged.

There is of necessity an intellectual component in this pursuit, but it is fruitful only if it results in increased likeness to Christ. Sincere moral effort in dependence on the Holy Spirit is involved.

Spiritual maturity is not the mere possession of spiritual gifts. The maturing Christian will have those spiritual gifts with which the Holy Spirit has sovereignly endowed him or her (see 1 Cor. 12:11), but these of themselves are not the measure of spiritual maturity. The case of the Corinthian church bears this out. Paul affirmed of them, "You do not lack any spiritual gift" (1 Cor. 1:7). Yet a little later he goes on to say to them, "Brothers, I could not address you as spiritual, but as worldly—mere infants in Christ. I gave you milk, not solid food, for you were not yet ready for it. Indeed, you are still not ready. You are still worldly" (1 Cor. 3:1–3a).

These spiritual gifts are valuable, but only if they are exercised in love and only as they result in the unity and upbuilding of the church. The true index of Christian maturity is not the possession of gifts of the Spirit, but the production of the fruit of the Spirit (see Gal. 5:22–23). It is sadly true that not all spiritually gifted believers act and react in a mature way.

The activity of the Holy Spirit in the believer bringing about progressive and manifest growth will always be the unimpeachable evidence that he is God's child. It may be possible for the gifts of the Spirit to be imitated in the context of a local culture, but Godlike quality of moral life called "the fruit of the Spirit"—its Spirit-led direction, its victory over the flesh—is the only valid evidence that one is God's child.

Spiritual maturity is not copying Christ. The Imitation of Christ by Thomas à Kempis does not advocate a self-generated copying of Christ. Spiritual maturity is rather what Paul said in 1 Corinthians 11:1, "Follow my example, as I follow the example of Christ." No one can live by the Sermon on the Mount, for example, without first experiencing the new birth and living it out under the control of the Holy Spirit. The steps of the Master are too majestic for unaided or unregenerate people to follow.

WHAT CHRISTIAN MATURITY IS

Before we can consider how to progress in spiritual maturity, we need to define several terms. The word frequently translated "perfect" in the King James Version of the Scripture is often and correctly rendered "mature" in more recent versions. Our English word "mature" is defined as "a state of full development."

The Greek word Paul uses, *teleios,* has a special technical meaning. It signifies "an end, a goal, a limit," and it combines dual ideas: first, the full development of one's powers; and second, the attainment of some goal or standard—the realization of the proper end of one's existence. So our word "mature" has come to mean complete or full grown, and implies ripeness in character and experience. It is used of the full development of adulthood as compared with the immaturity of childhood.

Philo divided his students into three categories: beginners, those who were making progress, and those who were beginning to attain maturity—classifications not unlike those of John who wrote to little children, young men, and fathers.

The word "perfect" or "mature" can be used of our Lord in the absolute sense, for during His life on earth all His powers reached their full development. He completely fulfilled His Father's will and attained the standard of perfection implied in His Father's will. He also attained the goal for which He came to earth—to redeem a world of lost men and women.

When the word "mature" is used of us, however, it is not absolute but relative; it is like comparing a child with an adult. The word "perfect" in the Book of Hebrews does not hold out the promise of moral perfection on earth. If that were attainable, how could we "keep on progressing toward maturity"? It has been pointed out that perfection always has another summit, but as the poet Coleridge said, "beyond what is found in Christ, the human race has not and will not progress."

To the Gnostics, "perfect" was a favorite and oft-used word. They used it to describe one who was no longer a novice, but one who had matured, was fully initiated, and had mastered the secrets of their own mystery religion. But as Marvin Vincent says, in Christ every believer is *teleios*—fully initiated into the most profound mysteries of the Christian gospel. As Paul used the term, it meant "mature and complete in Christ."

Viewed from another angle, spiritual maturity is simply *Christlikeness*. We are as mature as we are like Christ, and no more. He was the only fully mature man. His character was complete, well balanced, and perfectly integrated. All His qualities and capacities were perfectly attuned to the will of His Father, and this is the model, the standard God has set for us:

> It was he who gave some to be apostles, some to be prophets, some to be evangelists, and some to be pastors and teachers, to prepare God's people for works of service, so that the body of Christ may be built up, until we all reach unity in the faith and in the knowledge of the Son of God *and become mature, attaining to the whole measure of the fullness of Christ.* —Ephesians 4:11–13, italics mine

The supreme goal of the church is not evangelism, important and indispensable as that ministry is. The ultimate goal is stated by Paul when he wrote: "We proclaim him, teaching everyone with all wisdom, *so that we may present everyone perfect [mature] in Christ*" (Col. 1:28, italics mine). God's purpose is to produce disciples who reflect the perfect humanity of His Son, people who are able to react to the exigencies and trials of life in an adult and not in a childish manner—meeting adult situations with adult reactions. In short, God's purpose is to produce people who fulfill their humanity and become what God designed for them.

The questions naturally arise: "Can Christians attain a perfect maturity in this life? What degree of maturity can one expect?"

In his commentary, William Hendriksen says, "A high degree of maturity can be attained in this life here and now, but full maturity cannot be realized this side of heaven. In heaven we will be perfectly sinless and obedient."[1] This statement is in keeping with the whole tenor of Scripture:

> And we, who with unveiled faces all reflect the Lord's glory, are being transformed into his likeness *with ever-increasing glory,* which comes from the Lord, who is the Spirit. —2 Corinthians 3:18, italics mine

> Grow in the grace and in knowledge of our Lord and Savior Jesus Christ. —2 Peter 3:18

Maturity is not an end we have achieved. We are to keep on growing and progressing. "None of us has yet attained perfection. So come and take your full share in our gatherings and in our discussions, which are aimed at helping us all towards maturity. Don't stand aloof as though you know it all already."[2]

The above extract from *The Epistle of Barnabas* gives an insight into the thinking of one of the early church fathers. Because maturity is related to an infinite God, our maturity will never be absolute but only relative. It is a goal unattainable in this life, but it can be a dynamic process involving constant progress.

For the Christian, spiritual maturity involves a final transformation into the likeness of Christ, and this will be consummated at His second advent.

> Dear friends, now we are children of God, and what we will be has not yet been made known. But we know that when he appears, we shall be like him, for we shall see him as he is. Everyone who has this hope in him purifies himself, just as he is pure. —1 John 3:2–3

NOTES

1. William Hendriksen, *New Testament Commentary: Exposition of Ephesians* (Grand Rapids, Michigan: Baker Book House, 1967), p. 200.
2. Quoted in David Winter, *Faith Under Fire* (Wheaton, Illinois: Harold Shaw Publishers, 1977), p. 85.

3

Unduly Protracted Infancy

Brothers, I could not address you as spiritual but as worldly—mere infants in Christ. I gave you milk, not solid food, for you were not yet ready for it. Indeed, you are still not ready. —1 Corinthians 3:1–2

Until we all . . . become mature, attaining to the whole measure of the fullness of Christ. Then we will be no longer infants . . . blown here and there by every wind of teaching. —Ephesians 4:13–14

Anyone who lives on milk, being still an infant, is not acquainted with the teaching about righteousness. But solid food is for the mature. —Hebrews 5:13–14

"If I were called on to put my finger on the most pressing need of our age, I would unhesitatingly say— maturity." These words of an old preacher of the past are no less relevant in the wonder-world of the space age. It almost seems that as technology and knowledge advance, maturity recedes.

The low level of spiritual life in the Corinthian church occasioned acute distress for Paul. Their underlying problem was neither heresy nor apostasy but worldliness and spiritual immaturity. For the length of time they had been in possession of the truth, they should have been mature Christians. But to his dismay Paul discovered that they were still plagued with carnality. As a church they had been endowed not only with spiritual blessings but also with every spiritual gift. "You do not lack any spiritual gift," he told them (1 Cor. 1:7).

The Corinthian believers seemed to have a penchant for the spectacular and flamboyant, but they failed to evidence a maturity matching their gifts and claims. They majored in the exercise of the gifts of the Spirit, but they were sadly deficient in the fruit of the Spirit. Consequently the apostle had to tell them, "I could not address you as spiritual but as worldly—mere infants in Christ" (1 Cor. 3:1). In some way their spiritual growth had been arrested, and their legitimate spiritual infancy had become unduly protracted.

This problem is by no means confined to the early church; it is a major concern in many churches in our own day. There are too many adult-infants in our church rolls.

Should the pastor venture to launch into teaching some of the deeper truths of Scripture, a section of his congregation will complain that he is preaching over their heads. So he is on the horns of a dilemma. If he continues to feed them on little else than the milk of the Word, he leaves behind the more mature section of his congregation, while the others remain spiritual infants.

Paul stated the final objective of preaching in an exceedingly important verse that epitomizes the goal of the ministry of the Word: "We proclaim him, admonishing and teaching everyone with all wisdom, *so that we may present everyone perfect [mature] in Christ*. To this end I labor, struggling with all his energy, which so powerfully works within me" (Col. 1:28, italics mine). It will be the aim of the wise pastor to give teaching that will be relevant to people of all stages of spiritual development, and this is no easy task.

A LEGITIMATE SPIRITUAL INFANCY

The new life enters the new Christian in embryo form, and it must grow and develop as does an infant. For this desirable development to take place, congenial conditions for spiritual growth must be provided, and this is the responsibility of the one who disciples the new Christian. The environment and nourishment should be provided in the fellowship of the local church.

We often unintentionally discourage young Christians by entertaining unrealistic expectations. Every mother expects her baby to act and react like a baby. She does not look for adult behavior. Similarly we should be understanding and sympathetic with the early falls and struggles of a spiritual babe. In Hosea's prophecy, God is represented as acting in that way: "It was I who taught Ephraim to walk, taking them by the arms" (Hos. 11:3).

Within the right limits, babyhood is magic, but when it is unduly prolonged, it becomes tragic. It is wonderful to be a baby, but it is disastrous to remain one. It is to believers in this condition that Paul refers in the passages at the head of this chapter.

The Greek term used to describe this immature state is *sarchikos,* variously translated as "carnal," "men of flesh," and "worldly." Each rendering throws light on the meaning of the word, but the combination of the three makes an unhappy picture of the person in this state.

In Israel's memorable trek from the bondage of Egypt to the freedom of Canaan, we are given a divinely authorized illustration that is quite contemporary. Referring to this journey, Paul wrote, "Now these things occurred as examples, to keep us from setting our hearts on evil things as they did. . . . *These things happened to them as examples and were written down as warnings for us,* on whom the fulfillment of the ages has come" (1 Cor. 10:6, 11, italics mine). So we have biblical warrant for drawing spiritual lessons from Israel's history.

AN ILLEGITIMATE INFANCY

Once the Israelites had crossed the miraculously divided Red Sea, the journey into Canaan was only an eleven-day trek (Deut. 1:2). For wise reasons, however, God directed them to take a route that lengthened their travels by several months. This gave them time to adjust to their new and unaccustomed role as free people.

To reach Canaan, the Israelites had to cross the desert, and during the whole of this journey, they were walking in obedience to the will of God. This part of their trek was God-directed and therefore legitimate.

But once they reached Kadesh-Barnea, it was different. They rebelled against God and their leaders by despising and refusing to enter the Promised Land. This meant that the remainder of their desert wandering was contrary to the will of God and therefore illegitimate. The results were disastrous.

Israel's experience is duplicated in the lives of worldly Christians who do not go on to maturity. In a word, Paul's problem with the Corinthian church was worldliness. Their attitudes and reactions were worldly and not spiritual. They were fascinated by the more flamboyant spiritual gifts, while at the same time they tolerated grave abuses and open sin in their midst and allowed it to go unchecked. Envy, strife, party spirit, division, immorality, lawsuits between believers, and disorders at the Lord's table were all evidences of their carnal condition. They were "men of flesh," controlled not by the Spirit, but the self-life. Their spiritual immaturity was manifested in their reactions as well as their actions.

Our *actions* do not necessarily reveal our true motivation, for they can be insincere, superficial, even hypocritical. Our *reactions* to the unexpected, when we have had no time to prepare ourselves beforehand, are much more revealing and much more likely to be accurate. Spiritual immaturity is most clearly visible in our unrehearsed, unconscious reactions.

DIAGNOSIS OF SPIRITUAL IMMATURITY

The condition of the Corinthian church illustrates some of the traits of people who have failed to go on to maturity.

Arrested growth

The Corinthians had stopped growing and were static in their Christian experience—"mere infants in Christ," spiritual dwarfs. The main cause of their stunted condition was their feeble digestion. They could assimilate only the milk of the Word of God. Milk and meat are both divine provisions, but they are appropriate to different stages of the Christian life. Milk is the food suited to the infant, but "strong meat is for the mature."

Milk is predigested food that the babe receives secondhand from his or her mother, and the baby thrives on it. But the time comes when the child must be weaned and introduced to solids. The spiritually immature believer is one who has not been weaned from the "milk"—the elementary truths of the Word of God—but is still largely dependent for spiritual sustenance on the result of another's heart exercise and study of the Scriptures. The immature believer has never learned the art of drawing spiritual nourishment directly from his or her own study of Scripture and prayer. The spiritual babe has a poor digestion for unadorned Bible study and craves condiments to spice it up.

Unfortunately this craving is too often catered to, with the result that the spiritually immature person never progresses beyond a secondhand Christian experience. The spiritual infant is not able to stand on his or her own feet, but is unwilling to pay the price of serious Bible study in order to gain a firsthand knowledge of God and His Word.

It is possible for even an immature Christian to make rapid growth once such a purpose is formed and the motivation is sufficiently strong. Princess Diana of Britain confessed that she had to grow up quickly to deal with the pressures demanded by her new role as wife to the heir of the British throne. "I have learned a lot in the last few months," she said. "I have matured a lot recently and have got used to coping with things."[1] The motivation provided the rapid growth in maturity. A similar change has to take place in the life of one whose infancy has been unduly prolonged.

Emotional instability

Instability is shared by both an infant and an immature Christian. Paul describes the infantile stage as, "tossed back and forth by the waves, and blown here and there by every wind of teaching . . ." (Eph. 4:14). The immature Christian never reaches settled personal convictions so strong that he or she is willing to suffer for them.

The spiritually immature person tends to live in the realm of fickle emotions, and these can be both capricious and tyrannical. Instead of being motivated by the spiritual principles enunciated in the Scriptures, the spiritual infant is moved by transient feelings. In facing a decision, the question is not, "Will this please God?" but "Does this please me?" The person's actions are dictated more by how he or she feels about it than by what ought to be done. Like an infant, the spiritually immature person is a slave to feelings and thus lacks emotional stability. The spiritual infant should live more in the realm of the will, for we are what we choose, not what we feel.

Before Peter's transforming experience on the Day of Pentecost, he was a classic example of this emotional instability. One moment he was walking on the water, the next he was sinking beneath the waves. First he made his glorious confession of Christ's deity, then shortly afterward the Master had to rebuke him for his rash, Satan-inspired statement. Peter sincerely promised to lay down his life for his Lord, but a short time later he denied Christ three times.

After Pentecost, however, all this was changed. The marks of spiritual immaturity disappeared, and he became Peter the rock; he was no longer volatile but the stable, strong leader of the apostolic band.

Contentiousness

Most infants are very touchy, and their feelings are easily hurt. They have strong likes and dislikes and tend to be quarrelsome. These were qualities that came to the surface in the church at Corinth. "You are still worldly. For since there is jealousy and quarrelling among you, are you not worldly? Are you not acting like mere men?" (1 Cor. 3:3).

They had formed parties and cliques around their leaders instead of being united around Christ. "For when one says, 'I follow Paul,' and another, 'I follow Apollos,' are you not mere men?" (1 Cor. 3:4).

However competent the spiritually immature person may be in academic attainment or business acumen, it is usually this person who engages in contentious ecclesiastical politics and lobbying. The immature Christian will quarrel over minor matters or practice and procedure while important major spiritual issues are screaming for attention.

It is always Satan's strategy to polarize and divide believers and churches, and it is usually the immature Christian he enlists as his agent. The immature person creates problems; the mature person solves them.

Worldly-mindedness

"Are you not worldly?" Paul asked. "Are you not acting like ordinary men?" In other words, there was nothing in their behavior to distinguish them from others or to identify them as Christ's disciples. They appeared to be living on the same plane as those around them—conforming to the same standards, actuated by the same motives, dominated by the same desires. They were married to Christ yet flirting with the world. They were married to Christ yet not satisfied with Christ.

Insensitivity to evil

Inability to discriminate between good and evil is another mark of immaturity. The mature Christian is one who "by constant use has trained himself to distinguish good from evil"—that is, by constant consultation with the Word of God and obedience to its precepts.

The watchword of the immature person about doubtful things is, "What's the harm in it?" The mature Christian will ask rather, "What is the good in it?" The worldly person sees no harm in borderline things and usually acts according to desire rather than by principle. Because the thing the immature Christian desires to do is not specifically prohibited in Scripture, he or she is likely to engage in questionable practices. This lack of sensitivity to evil makes the spiritual infant an easy prey to the permissiveness that pervades society today.

Self-centeredness

An infant is self-centered and so is an immature believer. The current emphasis on loving oneself sounds rather strange when placed alongside our Lord's emphasis on denying oneself. The emphasis on loving oneself tends to be just another manifestation of spiritual infantilism. The mature person is self forgetful and spends love on others. The prayer of the mature Christian is:

Higher than the highest heaven,
Deeper than the deepest sea,
Lord Thy love at last has conquered;
Grant me now my heart's petition—
None of self, and all of Thee.
Theodore Monod, "None of Self"

The story is told that when Mahmoud, with his all-victorious armies, laid siege to Guzurat in India, he forced his way into the costliest shrine of the Brahmins. They prostrated themselves before him, offering vast ransom if only he would spare their god, for, they claimed, the fortunes of their city depended on him.

After a pause, Mahmoud replied that he would rather be known as the breaker than the seller of idols, and he struck the image with his battleaxe. It proved to be hollow and had been used as the receptacle for thousands of precious gems that, as the image was shattered, showered down at the conqueror's feet.

Such an idol is self. For Mahmoud to have spared the idol would have meant the sacrifice of untold wealth. To spare self spells spiritual penury. If we deliver the idol self to utter destruction at the hand of Christ, there will be showered upon us spiritual enrichment beyond our power to conceive.

But how can this tyrant—self—be ousted from the throne it has usurped? We are powerless to do it ourselves, for self cannot dethrone self. There is a more excellent way illustrated in the Old Testament story of a usurper, as recorded in 1 Kings 1:5–38.

How was Adonijah, the usurper of Solomon's crown, dethroned? By the enthronement of Solomon—which automatically achieved the *de*thronement of Adonijah. So the enthronement of Christ in the heart secures the dethronement of self, for two cannot occupy the throne at the same time.

"Let him deny himself," was our Lord's injunction to

His hearers, by which He meant, "Let him remove self from the center of authority." The verb is in the aorist tense, implying a crisis. It can take place in a moment of time. It will take place when, by an act of the will, we renounce the dominance of self, and with the Spirit's aid, place Christ on the throne of the heart.

For example, self-centeredness and selfishness are among the most prolific causes of marital disharmony. An experienced marriage counselor maintained that at the center of most marital problems is immaturity in either husband or wife—or in both. Where either partner is immature, their love is preponderantly physical and self-centered because they have failed to grow up emotionally and spiritually. Demanding love is immature love. Mature love is sacrificial and undemanding.

Destructive criticism

Destructive criticism is the mark of a carnal Christian. Its true character is seen in the fact that such criticism is always launched from a position of superiority. Very often the person who is overly ready to criticize others for their real or supposed faults and deficiencies is only seeking to compensate for his or her own very real faults. Such criticism is just the rebound of the person's own wrong attitudes.

It remains to be said that spiritual immaturity can coexist with great spiritual gifts. It is the fruit of the Spirit, not the gifts of the Spirit, that is the true evidence of spiritual maturity.

NOTES

1. New Zealand *Herald,* June 29, 1981.

4

Maturity Can Be Measured

It was he who gave some to be apostles, some to be prophets, some to be evangelists, and some to be pastors and teachers, to prepare God's people for works of service, so that the body of Christ might be built up until we all reach unity in the faith and in the knowledge of the Son of God and become mature, attaining to the whole measure of the fullness of Christ. *Then we shall be no longer infants.* —Ephesians 4:11–13, emphasis added

The biblical writers frequently draw parallels between physical and spiritual life, and in many cases the parallels are close. The physical maturity of a child can be measured with the aid of a tape measure and scales; the child's intellectual development can be gauged by examinations and tests. Likewise our own growth in maturity can be measured, and those most closely associated with us will be the best judges of our growth. Paul states the infallible standard of measurement—"the whole measure of the fullness of Christ."

This seems a daunting and unattainable standard; but then, could an infinitely holy and ethically perfect God entertain a standard any lower? Dr. A. T. Robertson, the eminent Greek scholar, throws light on this dilemma. In commenting on our Lord's staggering demand, "Be perfect therefore as your heavenly Father is perfect" (Matt. 5:48), he explains the significance of the word "perfect" in this context: "Here it is the goal set before us, the *absolute* standard of our heavenly Father. The word is also used for *relative* perfection, as of adults compared with children" (italics mine).[1]

We will know absolute maturity only when we see Christ and are like Him (see 1 John 3:2), but until then it is possible to attain a relative maturity, "continually progressing to maturity,"—the perfection of a child going on to maturity. Both aspects coalesce in Philippians 3:12–15, where Paul says,

> Not that I have already obtained all this, or have already been made perfect, but I press on to take hold of that for which Christ Jesus took hold of me. Brothers, I do not consider myself yet to have taken hold of it, But one thing I do: Forgetting what is behind and straining toward what is ahead, I press on toward the goal to win the prize for which God has called me heavenward in Christ Jesus. *All of us who are mature* should take such a view of things. (italics mine)

Paul here clearly disclaims having attained an absolute maturity, but he lays claim to a relative maturity in his experience.

HOW MAY WE GAUGE OUR DEGREE OF MATURITY?

Paul rules out the validity of comparing ourselves with ourselves. "We do not dare to classify or compare ourselves with some who commend themselves. When they measure themselves by themselves and compare themselves with themselves, they are not wise" (2 Cor. 10:12).

In his book *Christian Holiness* Bishop Stephen Neill

concurs with Paul's dictum. Bishop Neill writes, "Is man once again to be the measure of all things? By what standard am I to be judged? Is my unaided capacity at any one moment to be the measure at that moment of Christian attainment and Christian expectation?"[2]

The answer is, No! The measure of our maturity is seen when the "fullness of Christ"—the sum total of all the qualities that make Him what He is—is increasingly exhibited in our lives.

The primary mark of a developing maturity is growth in personal and experiential knowledge of God, coupled with a strong aspiration to know Him better. This was well illustrated in the experience of Moses. As his intimacy with God developed, he had the temerity to ask of Him, "If I have found favor in your eyes, teach me your ways so I may know you . . ." (Exod. 33:13). The readiness of the Lord's response should encourage others to make the same request. "And the Lord said to Moses, 'I will do the very thing you have asked . . .'" (Exod. 33:17a).

This gracious response gave Moses boldness to ask for yet a further blessing. Wonderful as it was to have an understanding of God's ways—the principles on which he governs His people—that only inflamed Moses' desire to know God himself in a more intimate way. So Moses asked, "Now show me your glory" (Exod. 33:18). This request, too, was granted. Every forward move toward a deeper knowledge of God was met by a positive response.

Paul cherished a similar aspiration. "I want to know Christ, and the power of his resurrection, and the fellowship in His sufferings, becoming like him in his death" (Phil. 3:10). Only a maturing Christian would share that aspiration. It was not a mere intellectual concept of Christ that Paul desired, but a comprehension, an acquaintance with Him on the deepest level that would issue in transformation and unreserved commitment.

The maturing Christian has as a life objective the

securing of the glory of God. The old Presbyterian catechism has its priorities right with its first question, "What is the chief end of man?" Equally right is its answer, "The chief end of man is to glorify God and enjoy Him for ever."

The first petition of Christ's pattern prayer, "Hallowed be your name," is really asking that God's name might be honored and glorified everywhere, by all people. If we prayed this petition sincerely, we could well add, "at any cost to me." Every choice in which the honor and glory of God is involved will have only one answer from the mature Christian. There is no room for debate.

After Jesus had opened His heart to His intimates in the Upper Room, he offered His moving High Priestly Prayer. The prayer sounds as if He is reporting to His Father about His earthly ministry: "I have brought you glory on earth by completing the work you gave me to do" (John 17:4). How concise yet how comprehensive! Since the servant is not greater than his or her Lord, the maturing Christian will experience a growing passion for the glory of God such as gripped Count Nikolaus von Zinzendorf, founder of the Moravian church—"I have one passion; it is He, He alone!"

To the mature Christian holiness will be more attractive than mere happiness. It seems that in some Christian circles, the pursuit of happiness has become almost pathological. In a recent letter from Dr. J. Hudson Taylor III, he makes the following assessment of the contemporary scene: "Ours is a very self-centered culture. Self-fulfillment and self-advancement have become our chief goals. Even Christians are not exempt from this. The leading question of our faith seems to be, 'How can I be happy and satisfied?' As a result there is shallow conversion and superficial commitment." The mature Christian has learned that true happiness is a by-product of holiness.

A consuming desire to be holy is clearer proof of

sanctification than is an itch for thrilling and exciting experiences. John Wesley once said he doubted that people had been made complete in Christ while they came to church to enjoy religion, instead of to learn how to be holy.

God wants His people to be joyous, and the Holy Spirit is the source of that fruit of the Spirit, which is joy. Jesus said, "These things have I spoken unto you, that my joy might remain in you, and that your joy might be full" (John 15:11 KJV). But true happiness comes only along the pathway of holiness.

Our Lord was the most joyous person this world has ever known, and this was because He was the holiest. It was said of Him, "You have loved righteousness and hated wickedness; therefore God, your *God, has set you above your companions by anointing you with the oil of joy*" (Heb. 1:9, italics mine).

When we make holiness the object of our pursuit, joy is thrown in as a bonus. It takes some of us a long time, however, to master the elementary lesson that we are happiest when we are holiest.

The maturing Christian becomes dissatisfied with the "milk" of the Word and craves "solid food." "You need milk," wrote the author of the letter to the Hebrews, "not solid food. Anyone who lives on milk, being still an infant, is not acquainted with the teaching of righteousness. But solid food is for the mature . . ." (Heb. 5:13a–14, italics mine).

No longer is the maturing Christian solely dependent on pre-digested spiritual food and artificial stimuli. The spiritual infant has now learned how to nurture the inner life on the Word of God and delves more deeply into its teachings. While enjoying helpful and challenging Christian literature, the main stimulus comes directly from the Word of God illuminated by the Holy Spirit.

The maturing Christian also has a growing discern-

ment that helps him to discriminate between truth and error, good and evil. "The mature ... by constant use have trained themselves to distinguish good from evil" (Heb. 5:14). There is such a thing as spiritual intuition, but more than that is in view here. It is a spiritual sensitivity that comes from "training"—that is, through the mastery of the principles of Scripture and their consistent application to the decisions and events of daily life.

This quality characterized the Christians at Berea. When new teaching was presented to them, they did not accept it on the mere say-so of those who brought it, but they searched the Scriptures daily to see if these things were really so. They trained their spiritual senses to detect error just as police dogs are trained to detect harmful drugs. The Bereans were not heresy hunters but truth seekers. This type of Christian does not fall an easy prey to the heresies and cults that abound today.

Like the Master, the maturing Christian prefers serving others to being served by others. The maturing Christian emulates the Lord who claimed, "I am among you as one who serves" (Luke 22:27c). "For even the Son of Man did not come to be served, but to serve" (Mark 10:45).

True spiritual leadership springs not from a desire to rule but from a passion to serve. This exotic grace is not native to most of us, but the Master equated it with greatness. "Whoever wants to be great among you must be your servant" (Mark 10:43).

This was one of the most revolutionary concepts Jesus introduced into the religious world of His day. Now, as then, most want to be masters not servants, leaders not followers. Christ's view of His kingdom was a community of people characterized by serving one another and the needy world outside. Unlike in earthly realms, our status in His kingdom is to be judged by the number of people whom we serve, not by the number who serve us.

It was in the context of servanthood that Jesus said, "I have set you an example that you should do as I have done for you. I tell you the truth, no servant is greater than his master, nor is a messenger greater than the one who sent him" (John 13:15–16).

The life of the maturing Christian will be characterized by giving rather than receiving. In this the Master is again the model. "The Son of Man [came] . . . to give his life as a ransom for many" (Mark 10:45). This, too, is not natural to us. In the Christian life we are mostly on the receiving end, but Jesus exemplified our responsibility to give as well as to receive.

From Bethlehem to Calvary, the Lord's life was one consistent giving of Himself, a constant outpouring of His life, until at its close, He gave up life itself. Every act of service He performed cost Him something. When an afflicted woman pressed her way through the throng and touched the fringe of His robe, she was healed. But in the process He lost something—nervous and spiritual force. "I know that power has gone out from me," Jesus said (Luke 8:46). He gladly gave of Himself to needy people in life, even as He gave His life for needy people in death.

It is far easier for us to give time or money than it is to give our very selves to those in need around us, yet this is the path to spiritual fruitfulness.

The mature Christian life will be fruitful, not barren. The ability to reproduce oneself is the proof of physical maturity, and this is also true of spiritual maturity. One of Christ's purposes for us as His disciples is that our lives should be fruitful. "You did not choose me, but I chose you to go and bear fruit—fruit that will last [. . . This is my command]" (John 15:16). A fruitless disciple is a contradiction in terms.

What constitutes "fruit"? We can look for it in two areas.

There will be *fruit in character*—the fruit of the Spirit

that finds expression in the nine winsome graces enumerated in Galatians 5:22–23. Note that these are passive rather than active qualities. All nine can be produced in the life of one who is paralyzed from the neck down. As we grow in maturity, these graces will be manifested in increasing measure.

There will be *fruit in service.* "Even now the reaper . . . harvests the crop for eternal life, so that the sower and the reaper may be glad together" (John 4:36). In writing to the Romans, Paul revealed the purpose of his visit: "I planned many times to come to you . . . in order that I might have a harvest among you" (Rom. 1:13). Souls won and lives discipled and encouraged into a closer walk with God will be evidence of a believer's growing maturity.

The maturing Christian's life will be dynamic rather than static. The growing believer will not resist change that is obviously in the interests of the church of God. The maturing Christian will reach out toward new horizons of service and will grapple with new concepts of truth. The growing believer will not be content with reading what is superficial but will welcome mind-stretching and heart-warming new aspects of truth. Growth will continue even in old age.

The maturing believer will accept rather than resent or rebel against the disciplines God in His wisdom allows to come into his or her life. If we are maturing as Christians, we may not actually enjoy the experience while we are passing through it—and Scripture realistically recognizes this possibility (see Heb. 12:11)—but we will regard the will of God as being "good, acceptable, and perfect" (Rom. 12:2 KJV), a statement that indicates that God's will for our lives cannot be improved upon.

As Paul's character matured, he was able to testify that he had reached the place where he could truthfully say, "I have learned to be content whatever the circumstances" (Phil. 4:11). Not that he had always been content, but his increasingly intimate walk with God had made him absolutely satisfied that whatever God ordained was in his best interests.

When tragedy, sorrow, or bereavement strike, it is not always easy to hold on to this contentment, but it is the only path to comfort and peace of heart. Paul enunciated a principle of perpetual relevance when he recorded the word from the Lord that came to him: "He said to me, 'My grace is sufficient for you, for my power is made perfect in weakness'" (2 Cor. 12:9).

He will glory in the Cross of Christ and will sing with Sir John Bowring:

> *In the cross of Christ I glory,*
> *Towering o'er the wrecks of time,*
> *All the light of sacred story*
> *Gathers round its head sublime.*

Only the spiritual person welcomes the impact of the Cross on his or her life, for it spells death to the self-life. "I have been crucified with Christ, and I no longer live, but Christ lives in me" (Gal. 2:20a).

The mature Christian will be willing to accept responsibility in the work of the kingdom. Not everyone is called to a place of prominence in God's service, but very many could do much more than they are doing if only they would respond to the promptings of the Spirit and the persuasion of godly people. All too many believers are content to be spectators instead of participators.

The immature Christian is content to accept all the blessings and benefits of faith but is unwilling to share the accompanying responsibilities. When God called Moses to lead Israel out of Egypt, he produced all kinds of excuses to cover up his unwillingness to assume that onerous responsibility. We can all understand and perhaps condone Moses' reluctance, but God did not. He was angry at Moses' lack of confidence that He would enable him to do what He had commanded (see Exod. 4:14). God is equally displeased with us when we decline responsibility and cover it up with a plea of inadequacy.

The mature believer will be willing to accept responsibility for failure, too, and will not shuffle the blame onto a subordinate.

The mature Christian will demonstrate a growing love for God and others. Paul commended the Thessalonian believers for this mark of their growing maturity: "We ought always to thank God for you, brothers, and rightly so, because your faith is growing more and more, and the love every one of you has for each other is increasing" (2 Thess. 1:3).

By pouring out his love into our hearts by the Holy Spirit (Rom. 5:5), God stimulates and enlarges our hearts and enables us to love Him in return. Love begets love. But when love cools, every grace languishes.

Growth in maturity is stimulated by sharing the knowledge of God with other believers, for we are to become mature in community life as well as in individual experience.

Paul talks of attaining "the unity of faith" as well as spiritual maturity, for that develops best not in isolation but in the corporate life of the church (see Eph. 4:13). This unity among believers is produced by their mutual sharing of "the knowledge of the Son of God"—an increasing acquaintance with Him in corporate life. F. F. Bruce rightly contends that "the higher reaches of the Christian life cannot be attained in isolation from others."[3] It is the team that is fully integrated and works together unselfishly and harmoniously that wins the game.

NOTES

1. A. T. Robertson, *Word Pictures in the New Testament I* (New York: R. R. Smith, Inc., 1930), p. 49.

2. Stephen Neill, *Christian Holiness* (New York: Harper & Row Publishers, 1960), p. 38.
3. Frederick F. Bruce, *Epistle to the Ephesians* (Old Tappan, New Jersey: Fleming H. Revell Co., 1961), p. 86.

5

The Function of Faith in Maturity

Now faith is being sure of what we hope for and certain of what we do not see. . . . Without faith it is impossible to please God, because anyone who comes to him must believe that he exists and that he rewards those who earnestly seek him. —Hebrews 11:1, 6

The stark absoluteness of the assertion that without faith it is impossible to please God is almost overwhelming in its implications. *Difficult* to please God? Yes, but surely not impossible! But there is no way of escaping the sweeping assertion.

Since this is the case, faith must be a tremendously important element in progressing toward maturity. It follows that a person of weak faith is also deficient in maturity, and vice versa.

Faith is confidence, reliance, trust. It is the sixth sense that enables one to apprehend the invisible but very real spiritual realm. Faith is confidence reposed in a God who is absolutely trustworthy, utterly reliable.

Faith is also an indispensable element in a walk in fellowship with God—a childlike, effortless trust that is never betrayed. Faith enables the believer to treat the future as present and invisible as seen. Faith is as much at home in the realm of the impossible as of the possible, since its reliance is on a God who knows no limitations, a God with whom all things are possible.

Faith does not exist apart from the object on which it is focused. It is akin to eyesight, which does not exist apart from the object of vision. In looking at something, we do not see our eyesight, but we see the object on which our vision is focused. So it is with faith.

The object on which faith relies is *not our faith* but that which enables us to see. It is our invisible link with God. Our responsibility is not so much to concentrate attention on our faith as to concentrate on Him to whom we look by faith. Jesus alone is the sinner's Savior; faith is simply the eye that looks to Him and apprehends Him in that role.

Faith is not merely a subjective state of mind, for there is always a corresponding objective fact to which it gives substance. "Now faith is the assurance of things hoped for, the conviction of things not seen" (Heb. 11:1 RSV). Faith is not merely passive. Every genuine act of faith is followed by an activity of faith. We do something about our assurance and conviction. Faith grows and develops with exercise but atrophies through neglect.

WALKING BY FAITH, NOT BY SIGHT

One distinction of a mature Christian is that he or she walks by faith, not by sight (see 2 Cor. 5:7)—two principles that are contradictory and mutually exclusive. Craving for outward signs or inward feelings rather than being a mark of deep spirituality, is evidence of spiritual immaturity. Jesus said in this connection, "Blessed are those who have not seen and yet have believed" (John 20:29b).

It is written of Abraham, the father of the faithful, that he looked away from earthly dwelling places and directed his gaze to "the city with foundations, whose architect and builder is God" (Heb. 11:10). Moses turned his back on earthly pomp and splendor and "endured, as seeing him who is invisible" (Heb. 11:27). Because of their implicit trust in God and in the reality of things unseen, both Moses and Abraham were invested with the order of faith, and their portraits were hung in God's "Gallery of Fame."

Much distress in the lives of immature Christians stems from an unresolved conflict between these two principles—faith and sight. Sight is concerned with the visible and tangible; faith is occupied with the invisible and spiritual. Sight is worldly prudence; faith is otherworldly wisdom. Sight concedes reality only to things present and seen; "faith forms a solid ground for what is hoped for, a conviction of unseen realities" (Heb. 11:1 BERKELEY). Each principle strives for ascendancy, and the believer chooses which will dominate his or her life.

The testing circumstances of life afford us the opportunity of adopting one principle or the other as a rule of life and action. Simon Peter was in large measure governed by sight and feeling before his maturing experience at Pentecost. Thereafter faith became the dominant principle of his life.

Note that faith is said to be "the *confidence* of things not seen," not the *consciousness* of things not seen. Before we can feel them, we must exercise faith in them. Faith is the initial act, feeling the resulting effect. Faith must recognize before it can realize, for feelings spring from facts. And the facts that impart stability to faith are those revealed in the promises and declarations of Scripture.

Feelings of joy are the outcome of believing joyful facts. Of course the facts remain unchanged whether we believe them or not, but our disbelief deprives us of their enjoyment.

It is possible that we often put more credence in our changing feelings than in the revealed facts of God's Word. In doing this, we not only cheat ourselves out of blessing, but, in effect, we make God a liar.

REVELATION AND REALIZATION

A divine progression in the activity of faith is seen in Romans 6:6, 11, 14. First comes the *revelation* of an objective fact, which is not dependent on any subjective feelings:

> We know that our old self was crucified with him so that the body of sin might be rendered powerless, that we should no longer be slaves to sin. —Romans 6:6

Next comes faith's *recognition* of the fact:

> In the same way, count yourselves to be dead to sin but alive to God in Christ Jesus. —Romans 6:11

Then follows the *realization,* the experience, the feeling based on the fact:

> Sin shall not be your master, because you are not under law, but under grace. —Romans 6:14

Faith is not produced by introspection—the perpetual taking of one's spiritual pulse. Instead, "Faith comes from hearing the message, and the message is heard through the word of Christ" (Rom. 10:17). Physicians say that a constant taking note of one's heartbeats tends to induce disorders of the heart. Faith flourishes best when it is focused on what God is and what He has said, not on one's feelings.

It is essential that the correct sequence be observed in this matter. If we desire to have a greater faith, we must discover a divinely authenticated fact on which it can rest. If we wish to enjoy feelings such as joy and peace, we must have faith in the facts on which joy and peace are based. Then we can expect to be filled "with all joy and peace in believing" (Rom. 15:13).

DEGREES OF FAITH

Faith may operate on several planes, for not all Christians exercise faith to the same degree in testing circumstances.

"Why are you so afraid?" Jesus asked His disciples in the midst of a frightening storm. "Do you still have no faith?" (Mark 4:40). Unbelief has a very short memory. The disciples' fear and lack of faith caused them to forget His past miraculous interventions on their behalf; lack of faith made them doubt His loving concern for their welfare. In the face of superhuman difficulties, unbelief gives way to despair.

When Peter began to sink in the engulfing waves, Jesus said to him, "You of little faith . . . , why did you doubt?" (Matt. 14:31). On another occasion Christ rebuked His followers with, "O you of little faith" (Matt. 6:30). The unmistakable inference is that worry and anxious care spring from an anemic faith.

Peter had begun his walk on the unstable waves as an act of faith. But when he turned his gaze away from his omnipotent Lord to the billowing waves, when he reverted to the principle of sight, he *sank*. We will always sink when we prefer sight to faith. Christ appreciates a faith that ignores sight and boldly steps out upon His sure word of promise.

Great faith obtains whatever it will from God when the thing desired is sanctioned by Scripture or borne witness to by the Holy Spirit. To the woman of Canaan Jesus said, "Woman, you have *great faith!* Your request is granted" (Matt. 15:28, italics mine).

In this account, the woman's great faith enabled her to overleap the *silence* of the Lord (v. 23). It overcame His *apparent exclusivism* (v. 24). It overlooked his apparent *severity* (v. 26). So gladdened and impressed was the Master at the triumph of her great faith that He gave her all she asked.

"Seeing is believing," says the worldly-wise person. "Believing is seeing," affirms the person of mature faith. The Bible abounds in such paradox—something apparently wrong and contrary to reason yet actually true. Biblical teaching on the subject of faith is often cloaked in paradox, as in our Lord teaching that the grain of wheat was dead because it had not died (see John 12:24).

FAITH SINGS IN PRISON

Paradoxically, too, faith sings while still in prison. Its song of praise antedates its release, as in the case of Paul and Silas (see Acts 16:25). Faith can fight effectively even when bound in chains (see 2 Tim. 2:9).

Faith can flourish in the midst of trial and tragedy, but it will not purchase immunity from these experiences for the Christian. The prophet Habakkuk affords a shining example of the triumph of faith under fire. Stationed on his rural watchtower, he was perplexed by the dual problem of unanswered prayer and an apparently inactive Providence. The prosperity of the wicked and the afflictions of the righteous seemed inconsistent with his conception of God's nature.

Relief came when Habakkuk received a word from the Lord—"the righteous will live by his faith" (Hab. 2:4). With this assurance, he was able to meet stark tragedy with a song in his heart. Hear the sublime strains of his faith:

> Though the fig tree does not bud and there are no grapes on the vines, though the olive crop fails and the fields produce no food, though there are no sheep in the pen and no cattle in the stalls, *yet will I rejoice in the Lord, I will be joyful* in God my Savior.
> —Habakkuk 3:17–18, italics mine

Because the prophet had God, he had all, and through his faith in God, he was able to face and survive even tragedy and heartbreak.

The spiritually mature Christian experiences *the rest of faith*. While faith inspires the most intense activity, paradoxically it also induces the most complete heart-rest. "There remains, then, a sabbath-rest for the people of God" (Heb. 4:9). "Now we who have believed do enter that rest" (Heb. 4:3). It was lack of faith that hindered God's people from experiencing the rest of the Promised Land, and unbelief has the same baneful effects today.

This rest of faith is attained when the soul is brought by the Holy Spirit into the place of complete adjustment to the will of God. When two wills are in conflict, there can be no rest.

This rest of faith is not one of inaction but one of harmony with the will of God. When we thus rest in Christ, we transfer the whole weight of our responsibility and care to Him; we allow Him to bear it, as Peter exhorts: "Cast all your anxiety on him because he cares for you" (1 Pet. 5:7).

THE OMNIPOTENCE OF FAITH

Dare we suggest that faith can enjoy even a sort of omnipotence? Did not our Lord say to the father of the demon-possessed boy, "Everything is possible for him who believes"? (Mark 9:23b). Had these words fallen from the lips of someone other than the Son of God, they could with reason be dismissed as sheer fantasy. But Christ spoke them as a plain statement of fact. Of course this does not mean that one can use faith to gratify every whim and desire; but it does mean that the person of faith can do and have anything that is within the will of God, no matter how seemingly impossible. It is impossible, however, for anyone to exercise faith in God for what is outside the will of God.

Faith functions in cooperation with God. When Jesus uttered that cryptic statement, "It is easier for a camel to go through the eye of a needle than for a rich man to enter the kingdom of God," it is recorded that "the disciples were even more amazed, and said to each other, 'Who then can be saved?' Jesus looked at them and said, 'With man this is impossible, but not with God; all things are possible with God'" (Mark 10:25–27).

Note that our Lord did not say, "*to* God all things are possible," but "*with* God all things are possible." "To God" would underline the contrast between our impotence and God's omnipotence. But to the believer "with God," united by faith to God, all things are possible.

Samuel Chadwick, the great Methodist stalwart, declared that with God and for the Will of God, the Christian is almighty. And with God, all that a person ought to be, he or she can be; and all that person ought to do, he or she can do.

> *'Twas most impossible of all*
> *That here in me sin's reign should cease;*
> *Yet shall it be? I know it shall,*
> *'Tis certain though impossible.*
> *The thing impossible shall be,*
> *All things are possible to me!*

Charles Wesley

Is this concept not confirmed by Paul's affirmation: "I can do everything through Him, who gives me strength"? (Phil. 4:13). It accords also with Augustine's prayer: "Give what Thou commandest, then command what Thou wilt."

FAITH AND THE PROMISES

Faith feeds on the promises of God. The conscious presence of God is the atmosphere in which faith thrives.

But in the malarial swamps of our doubts and questionings, faith wilts and dies.

Faith develops best when all props are removed, for the exercise of faith always involves taking a risk. Where no risk is involved, faith is unnecessary. It increases as it responds to the requirements and challenges of the Word of God. Contrary to popular belief, faith is not always fostered best by great encouragements and swift answers to prayer, much as we appreciate them. Faith thrives more in the midst of difficulties and conflicts, when all secondary supports have been removed.

Faith grows with greatest speed when we believe our beliefs and doubt our doubts. The surest way to arrest its growth is to doubt our beliefs and believe our doubts. Faith always involves an act of the will, and we must choose the path we will pursue, the high road or the low.

> *Faith, mighty faith the promise sees,*
> *And looks to God alone,*
> *Laughs at impossibilities,*
> *And cries it shall be done!*
>
> Charles Wesley

THE ACTIVITY OF FAITH

It is written of the heroes of faith that through faith they conquered kingdoms, shut the mouths of lions, quenched the fury of the flames and escaped the edge of the sword (see Heb. 11:33–34).

Faith is not passive and inactive, a state of pious moral indolence. Rather it is the inspiring secret of intense activity. There was no passivity in the saints to whom these achievements were credited. Their faith was the motivating factor in their magnificent exploits. A similar vital faith on our part will move us to attempt great things for God.

On the other hand, unbelief shackles omnipotence. When Jesus returned to His own town, we read "He could not do any miracles there. . . . And he was amazed at their lack of faith" (Mark 6:5–6). Note the "could not"—it was a moral and spiritual impossibility, not a physical impossibility. This incident lends credibility to John Wesley's contention that "God does nothing except in answer to believing prayer." Jesus was ever so willing to perform acts of mercy among these people, but the sole channel through which His healing power could flow was blocked. Could it be that often the seeming inactivity of God is due to our unbelief?

Faith is frequently called on to run in double harness with patience. It is in this school that faith is matured. We are counseled to follow those who "through faith and patience received the promise." Faith grows and matures through being tested. Waiting often seems more difficult than believing. But if the waiting is joined to unwavering faith, we will prove without fail that God "acts on behalf of those who wait for him" (Isa. 64:4).

6

No Maturity
Without Discipleship

"If you continue in my word, you are truly my disciples." —John 8:31 RSV

"All men will know that you are my disciples if you love one another." —John 13:35

"By this is my Father glorified, that you bear much fruit, and so prove to be my disciples." —John 15:8 RSV

Discipleship and spiritual maturity go hand in hand. The mature Christian will understand the principles of discipleship and will bring his or her life into conformity with the conditions so clearly enunciated by the Master.

It is significant that Jesus did not command His followers to go and make *believers* of all nations. His words were, "Go and make *disciples* of all nations" (Matt. 28:19a). A disciple is a learner who accepts the teachings of a tutor not only in belief but also in life. A disciple accepts in a realistic and practical way the views and practices of the teacher.

When J. Edgar Hoover was head of the Federal Bureau of Investigation, a young communist whom he was interviewing volunteered this statement: "We communists do not learn in order to demonstrate what a high I.Q. we have. *We learn in order to put into practice what we have learned*" (italics mine). It is this factor that marks the difference between a mere believer and a true disciple of Christ. It is of the essence of real discipleship.

Christians can learn from the Communist party, which requires of every member an absolute commitment. Nikita Kruschev asserted, "In communism we have no spectators." This is more than we can claim for the church. Lenin declared that they would not accept into membership anyone who entertained any reservation whatsoever. Only active, disciplined members of one of their organizations were admitted.

When we respond to Christ's call to discipleship, we enter His school and place ourselves under His instruction. His teaching manual is the Bible, the source book in which all His instruction is rooted.

Originally, "Christian" and "disciple" were interchangeable terms, but that is far from the case today. Many who profess to be Christians are quite unwilling to comply with Christ's conditions of discipleship as set out, for example, in Luke 14:25–35. In the early church, discipleship often involved an actual sharing of the treatment that the world meted out to Christ. For some it meant the dreaded cry, "Christians to the lions!"

Jesus never led His disciples to believe that the path of discipleship would be easy. He was too honest and sincere for that. He clearly indicated the cost involved, for He was seeking quality more than quantity among His followers. In His battle with the powers of darkness, He needed men and women whose eyes were open to the inevitable repercussions.

Robert Browning understood the high cost of following Christ when he wrote these lines:

> *How very hard it is to be a Christian!*
> *Hard for you and me;*
> *Not the mere task of making real*

> *That duty up to its ideal,*
> *Effecting thus complete and whole*
> *A purpose of human soul,*
> *For that is always hard to do.*[1]

It was because the Lord made the terms of discipleship so exacting that He lost some of His followers. "On hearing it, many of His disciples said, 'This is a hard teaching. Who can accept it?' . . . From this time many of His disciples turned back and no longer followed him" (John 6:60, 66). True discipleship has never been popular, except with the mature.

In the course of His ministry, Jesus enunciated some fundamental principles to guide His followers in their life and service:

THE CONTINUANCE PRINCIPLE

> *Jesus then said to the Jews who had believed in him,* "If you continue in my word, *you are truly my* disciples, *and you will know the truth, and the truth will make you free.*" —John 3:31–32 RSV, emphasis mine

This gives the *inward* view of discipleship, the attitude of the pupil to the teacher—permanent continuance in the words of the Master. Where this element is absent, discipleship is merely nominal and lacks reality.

What did Jesus mean by the expression, "my word"? In a sense it is indistinguishable from the teacher Himself, for He is the living Word. The sense here, however, appears to be—the whole tenor and substance of His teaching. "My word" stands for His message as a whole, all He taught when on earth. Not just favorite passages or pet doctrines, but the whole range of His teaching.

Our Lord's conversation with the two disciples on the

Emmaus road is revealing in this connection: "Beginning with Moses and all the Prophets, he explained to them what was said in all the Scriptures concerning himself" (Luke 24:27).

To "continue in his word," or to "hold to his teaching," as it reads in the New International Version, meant to make it the rule of life and practice, and as a corollary, to obey it strictly. Discipleship begins with the reception of the Word, but Jesus made continuance in it the test of reality.

Columba was an evangelist who left his native Ireland to bring the gospel to Scotland. He realized that not only would he face great difficulties and opposition, but also he could be tempted to give up and return home. A mound on the beach where he buried his boat when he landed bore eloquent testimony to the reality of his purpose to obey his Lord's command to go and make disciples of all nations. A real disciple is one who has committed himself or herself to follow Christ without any reservations.

At a conference in Ben Lippen, South Carolina, a young woman gave her testimony. In doing so, she held up a sheet of paper stating that it contained God's will for her life, and she had accepted it. The only writing on the paper was her signature at the bottom. Then she said, "I have accepted God's will for my life without knowing what it is, and I am leaving it to Him to fill in the details." That was real discipleship. She was on safe ground. With such a yielded will, the Holy Spirit would assuredly be able to guide her mental processes when she periodically had to make decisions about her future.

Some people decide to follow Christ on impulse, making their decision on a wave of enthusiasm that too often proves short-lived. It was in view of such a possibility that Jesus, in a message on the cost of discipleship, gave a serious warning:

"Suppose one of you wants to build a tower. Will he not first sit down and estimate the cost *to see if he has enough money to complete it? For if he lays the foundation and is not able to finish, everyone who sees it will ridicule him saying, 'This fellow began to build and was not able to finish.'"* —Luke 14:28–30, emphasis mine

An impulsive decision often lacks the element of deep commitment, with the result that when its full implications are realized, the cost proves too great and the commitment is rescinded. Even during Christ's earthly ministry "many of his disciples turned back and no longer followed him" (John 6:66).

SHORT-TERM DISCIPLESHIP

Others are willing to follow Christ, but only on a short-term basis. The New Testament, however, makes no provision whatever for short-term discipleship. We live in days when most involvements are short term. This is becoming true even with the marriage covenant.

The location in which we exercise our discipleship may be for a short term, but total and long-term commitment is involved. Short-term disciples usually do not burn their bridges behind them. Short-term disciples do not bury their boats as Columba did. They seldom quite reach the point of no return.

A young man recently said to me, "I think I will take a trip to Asia and look around to see what it is like. If I feel comfortable about it, I might possibly return as a missionary." He was a short-term disciple. But the Great Commission does not make the comfort of the messenger the determining factor. One whose discipleship was so languid and calculating would be no asset to the missionary force.

Samuel Chadwick stated the implications of discipleship in terms that are stringent and rather daunting, but not more so than the Master's own words in Luke 14:26, 27, 33. Here are Chadwick's words:

> We are moved by the act of God. Omniscience holds no conference. Infinite authority leaves no room for compromise. Eternal love offers no explanations. The Lord expects to be trusted. He disturbs us at will. Human arrangements are disregarded, family ties ignored, business claims put aside. We are never asked if it is convenient.[2]

But having said that and recognizing the absolute Lordship of Christ, Chadwick's statement should be balanced by the fact that God is not only the sovereign Lord who does as He wills, but He is also a loving Father whose sovereignty will never clash with His paternity.

Isaiah highlighted this comforting truth when he wrote: "Yet, O Lord, you are our Father. We are the clay, you are the Potter; we are all the work of your hand" (Isa. 64:8). The Fatherhood of God is our guarantee that His sovereignty will never require of us or do to us anything that He sees will not, in the long run, be in our best interests.

Continuance in Christ's Word is not automatic. It is the result of strong purpose and self-discipline. It will involve taking time not only to read but also to meditate on God's Word—turning it over in the mind in much the same way as a cow chews the cud. It will include memorization of certain portions—hiding God's Word in our hearts.

To be productive, reading and meditation will need to be "mixed with faith," for without this there will be little profit. It was written of the ancient Israelites, "The message they heard was of no value to them, because those who heard it did not combine it with faith" (Heb. 4:2b).

But even reading, meditation, and faith have small value if they are not followed by obedience to the truths learned. It is when we keep His commandments that we demonstrate the reality of our discipleship.

THE LOVE PRINCIPLE

> *"A new commandment I give you: Love one another. As I have loved you, so you must love one another.* All men will know that you are my disciples *if you love one another." —*John 13:34–35, emphasis mine

This verse gives the *outward* view of discipleship and involves our relations to others.

On Saturday evenings it was the custom of Samuel Rutherford, the godly Scottish minister, to prepare his family for the Lord's day by reading them their catechism. Questions and answers went around the table.

One Saturday evening this exercise was disturbed by a knock at the door. The hospitable Rutherford invited the stranger to join the family circle.

When the stranger's turn to answer came, his question was, "How many commandments are there?"

"Eleven," replied the stranger.

Rutherford was surprised that such an obviously well-educated man should be so ignorant, so he corrected him. But the stranger justified his answer by quoting: "A new command I give you: Love one another."

The stranger accepted hospitality for the night. Next morning, as the minister was walking to the church, he heard from behind the hedge a voice raised in prayer, and recognized the voice of the stranger. It was a wonderful prayer and Rutherford waited until the stranger emerged. "Who are you?" he inquired.

"I am Archbishop Ussher, Primate of Ireland," was the reply. "I had heard so much about your piety that I took this method of finding out for myself."

Their hearts flowed together in common devotion. The archbishop was invited to speak, and not surprisingly, the text he chose was, "A new command I give you: Love one another."

We are not to love others merely because we like them. Aversion and affinity are alike irrelevant. Our love must not be selective because of family or social ties. We should not love others because they are neighbors geographically, but simply because being redeemed sinners ourselves, we seek to share the love of Christ with them.

Jesus told us we are to love others even as He loved us. How did He express His love?

His was *selfless love*. Even in the noblest human love there is always some element of self-interest. We love, in part, because of what it brings to us, the happiness it imparts. Christ's love was unconditional, unselfish, and disinterested in what it received in return.

It was *forgiving love*. The only one in a position to forgive is the one against whom the offense has been committed. Although our Lord was doubted, denied, betrayed, forsaken, His love was not quenched. When He told Peter that his forgiveness was to extend, not to seven offenses but to seventy times seven, He was only illustrating the extent of His own forgiving love for His failing followers.

It was *sacrificial love*. Every act of service that the Lord performed cost Him something. As mentioned earlier, when He forgave the woman who pressed through the crowd to touch the fringe of His garment, it is recorded that "Jesus realized that power had gone out from him" (Mark 5:30). There was no limit to sacrifices He was prepared to make in His lifetime, but the supreme sacrifice was made when He died on the cross. True love gives unconditionally and demands nothing in return.

This is the paramount principle of discipleship. Genuine love for one another is the finally authentic mark. When people see this evidence, they will say, "These are true disciples of Christ. We can see it by the warmth of their love for one another."We can preach and pray, we can give sacrificially and witness faithfully, but without this love as the inspiring motive, we gain nothing, we are spiritual nonentities (see 1 Cor. 13:1–3).

·THE FRUIT PRINCIPLE

> *"If you remain in me and my words remain in you, ask whatever you wish, and it will be given you, this is to my Father's glory, that you bear much fruit, showing yourselves to be my disciples."* —John 15:7, emphasis mine

This passage shows the *upward* view of discipleship. A fruitless disciple is a contradiction in terms. If there is no real spiritual fruit in our lives, we are not real disciples.

What constitutes "fruit"? Primarily, the fruit mentioned here is for God and His glory, and only in a secondary sense is it for us. The fruit is manifested in two areas. As previously stated, it is first of all *fruit in character*—in the inward life (see Gal. 5:22–23). The evidence of the Holy Spirit's work in our lives is expressed in nine winsome graces, each of which was seen in perfection in the life of Christ. The tree is known by its fruit. The disciple is recognized by his or her likeness to Christ in inward character.

In addition to fruit in character, true discipleship will bear *fruit in service*—in outward ministry. This fruit is seen when men and women are won to Christ, when converts are discipled by other concerned disciples, and when Christians are led on to spiritual maturity.

It remains to be said that fruit bearing, a mark of true discipleship, is not automatic. Fruit bearing is optional.

Jesus made this clear when He said, "I tell you the truth, unless a kernel of wheat falls into the ground and dies, it remains only a single seed. *But if it dies,* it produces many seeds" (John 12:24, italics mine).

Jesus thus linked fruit bearing with the Cross. And did He not exemplify this truth in His own death? The single kernel of wheat that fell into the ground and died on Calvary produced three thousand seeds fifty days later at Pentecost; and His death has continued to produce them in ever-increasing numbers ever since.

The operative words in John 12:24 are: "unless" and "if." The glorious possibility of abundant fruitfulness lies in our own hands. "It is enough for the student to be like his teacher, and the servant like his master" (Matt. 10:28). The onus for fruit-bearing is placed squarely on our own shoulders.

> *Which shall it be, little corn of wheat?*
> *Do you choose to live as a golden seed,*
> *Or die alone in an earthen bed*
> *For the hungry world in need?*
>
> *Will you save your life from the cold and rain,*
> *Or give it back to the furrowed field,*
> *The soon the reaper's hands may come*
> *And gather the harvest yield?*
>
> *Which shall it be, O soul of mine?*
> *Will you love your life for a few short years,*
> *Or give it all for the Master's sake*
> *And the cry of the world through tears?*
>
> *Though you lose your life, it will spring anew*
> *From the tomb where it once was sealed,*
> *And a wealth of golden sheaves shall stand*
> *In the Master's harvest field.*
>
> Ruth Gibbs Zwall

NOTES

1. As quoted in S. M. Zwemer, *It is Hard To Be a Christian* (London: Marshall, Morgan & Scott, n.d.), p. 15.
2. Noted in text but no information.

7

Age Not Equated
With Maturity

*Since my youth, O God, you have taught me, and to
this day I declare your marvelous deeds. Even when I
am old and gray, do not forsake me, O God, till I
declare your power to the next generation, your might
to all who are to come.* —Psalm 71:17–18

"I'm only as old as my attitudes, not my arteries,"
declared a sanguine old man. It is altogether too optimistic
an assessment of the situation to equate old age with
maturity. They are by no means married to each other. It
would be ideal if all old people were mature, but the ideal is
not always realized. In fact, the reactions of some elderly
people are the very reverse of mature. It is not our
chronological age but our attitudes that determine the
degree of our maturity.

Because people differ so widely in background, temperament, and outlook, attitudes vary greatly. Some face
the prospect of growing old in a totally negative manner,
and as a result their reactions are set in a minor key. Others
entertain a more positive and sanguine outlook, and
accordingly they strike more major chords.

It is the latter group that evidences true spiritual
maturity. This is because they have embraced the liberat-
ing truth that the will of God—which includes old age—is
"good, acceptable, and perfect" (Rom. 12:2 KJV). They
take those words in their fullest and most literal sense as

being true, not only of Christians in general, but also of themselves in particular.

GOD'S WILL PERFECT AND ACCEPTABLE

Most Christians find it no insuperable problem to assent *theoretically* to the proposition that God's will is perfect and therefore cannot be improved on. But they find it something quite other to maintain with equal sincerity that it is acceptable to them as their powers wane, limitations increase, and strength begins to fail. And yet this is the only avenue open to faith. If God's will is indeed acceptable, it is to be accepted, and the mature reaction will be to accept it with thanksgiving.

When God's will is thus accepted from the heart, serenity ensues. Acceptance taps new sources of strength that enable one to rise above the limitations and handicaps that are all too real.

In its realistic approach to the less desirable accompaniments of the aging process, the Bible does not gloss them over but consistently presents the stark contrast between an old age lived in vital fellowship with God and old age lived without Him.

Paul faced life realistically as he grew old. "Though outwardly we are wasting away," he wrote, "yet inwardly we are being renewed day by day" (2 Cor. 4:16). Outward deterioration, inward renewal. The breaking up of the house of clay is not the whole story. Paul testified that along with the wasting of the body, a counter-process was also in progress. He received day by day fresh accessions of strength from God to enable him to meet the exigencies of each day. What Paul received from God, we can receive from the God who "gives strength to the weary and increases the power of the weak" (Isa. 40:29). According to our faith, so will it be to us.

The triumph of a mature attitude was seen in the life of Emma Piechynska, the wife of a sadistic Polish count. Her biographer described her reaction to her husband's tyranny in these words:

> There was no mournful resignation or melancholy submission about her. Every fresh experience of suffering was a challenge to her will. Suffering must not be accepted with mere submission. It must be borne deliberately. Every experience is worth what it costs.

A noble tribute was paid to the spirit in which she accepted her trials: "She made beautiful bouquets out of the refusals of God. Her life was enriched by the things that were withheld."[1]

ACCEPTING OUR AGE

If we are to experience joy and serenity in our closing years, we must gladly accept our age and what it brings as part of God's perfect will. We must deliberately and resolutely lay ourselves out to maintain a positive and cheerful outlook. Of course there can be a phony cheerfulness that is only a facade. But true "joy in the Holy Spirit" is a supernatural something that transcends even suffering, pain, and increasing limitation.

It should be our fixed ambition to make our last years the best—best for God, best for others, and best for ourselves. And why should they not be the best, freighted as they are with the wisdom of experience? Did not God promise, "I . . . will do better unto you than at your beginnings"? (Ezek. 36:11 KJV).

> *What then? Shall we sit idly down and say,*
> *The night is come; it is no longer day?*

> *For age is opportunity no less*
> *Than youth itself, though in another dress.*
> *And as the evening twilight fades away,*
> *The sky is filled with stars*
> *Invisible by day.*

H. W. Longfellow

When John Wesley was an old man, striking testimony was borne to the radiance of his personality. "Wherever he went, he diffused a portion of his own felicity. In him old age appeared delightful, like an evening without a cloud. And it was impossible to observe him without wishing, 'May my latter end be like his!'"

Some elderly folk fairly radiate joy, and their very presence is a benediction. They evidence an attractive maturity to which the self-absorbed and self-pitying are strangers.

A CONTINUING CONTRIBUTION

The aging Christian has so much to share with the coming generation; advancing years being a maturity of wisdom and a breadth of sympathy that cannot be gleaned from textbooks, but only in the school of life. The elderly Christian possesses a wisdom that has been hammered out, often painfully, on the anvil of experience. The aging Christian has the privilege and responsibility of making available to all who need and desire it, these dearly bought discoveries.

With less pressure of time, older people can, to a degree never before possible, discover afresh the joy of serious Bible study, of leisurely reading, of an orderly life of prayer that makes the world their parish.

"The influence of a Christian in old age is one of cumulative and peculiar power," said an old writer. "It gathers into itself the forces of long-tried character and is rich in ripened experience. The work a Christian does in the closing years of life often has a vitality in it which busier years had not." There is a great potential, largely untapped, in the accumulated experience, knowledge, and maturity of older Christians.

The exhortation of Hebrews 6:1 (WILLIAMS), "Let us keep on progressing toward maturity," encourages us to believe that growth and development can continue until the end of life. Medical specialists are united in maintaining that apart from serious illness or other adverse physical conditions, the normal human being can learn to grow at any age. The laws of mental and spiritual growth—if we are sufficiently motivated to apply them—will be operative right until the end of life, although the pace may be slower. Someone has said that we do not grow old with age, we age because we are not growing.

INWARD GROWTH STILL POSSIBLE

Despite our age and physical condition, we must keep growing spiritually. Inward growth is still possible after the physical body falls into decay, for all true growth is mental and spiritual. It is a widely accepted fact that as long as disease does not impair our mental faculties, mental activity can continue increasing even in old age.

When he was over eighty years of age, Arnold Toynbee, the British historian, wrote: "Our minds, so long as they keep their cutting edge, are not bound by physical limits; they can range over time and space into infinity."[2]

A Canadian member of the China Inland Mission (now the Overseas Missionary Fellowship), Benjamin Ririe, retired from missionary work in China at the age of seventy and settled in Toronto. When he was eighty, he decided to take up the study of New Testament Greek. He became proficient in reading the New Testament in that language.

At the age of ninety, he took a refresher course in Greek at a Baptist college in Toronto. When he had reached the age of one hundred, he attended a meeting at which I was the speaker. In his pocket was a well-worn Greek lexicon that he had used to brush up his Greek while he traveled on the subway across the city! At the age of one hundred he was still ambitious to be his intellectual best for God. Do we share that ambition, or are we content to allow our mental powers to atrophy? His example has something to say to older people who have ceased to expect and strive after mental growth in their later years. His was an example of maturity at its best.

NEVER TOO LATE

Abraham's progress toward maturity was marked by a series of crises. The first was God's call to Abraham to leave his comfortable and affluent ancestral home and embark on a nomadic lifestyle. He obediently set out on this exciting second career at the age of seventy-five (see Gen. 12:1).

Abraham certainly was no callow youth in search of adventure. It says much for his maturity—and that of his wife Sarah who was only ten years younger—that, as the record puts it, "By faith Abraham, when called to go to a place he would later receive as his inheritance, obeyed and went, even though he did not know where he was going" (Heb. 11:8).

Dietrich Bonhoeffer could have had Abraham in mind when he wrote, "It is the mark of a grown-up man as compared with a callow youth, that he finds his center of gravity wherever he happens to be at the moment. And however much he longs for the object of his desire, it cannot prevent him staying at this post and doing his duty." Abraham fully measured up to this standard.

It would have been a traumatic experience for a woman much younger than Sarah to break up her luxurious home. Ur of the Chaldees was a highly civilized city, and her husband was a wealthy man. To leave her treasures behind and take with her only such things as were appropriate to a nomadic tent-dwelling life must have created considerable apprehension. For comfortable city dwellers to so change their whole lifestyle at that time of life required faith and courage of a more than ordinary degree. In taking the tremendous first step, both Abraham and Sarah progressed a long way on the road to maturity.

Many stupendous achievements have been marked up by old and seriously handicapped people. Beethoven in music and Milton in literature triumphed gloriously over their age and limiting handicaps. These and others like them refused to be daunted by their physical disabilities, and to them the whole world is eternally indebted.

Beethoven composed some of his most glorious musical works toward the end of his life when he was completely deaf. Milton wrote some of his most magnificent poetry during his last years of blindness. The world would have been greatly impoverished had there been no Beethoven's *Ninth Symphony* and no *Paradise Lost*.

It was my privilege to share the ministry at a Navigators' conference with Dr. Herbert Lockyer. In spite of—or was it because of?—his ninety-two years, he delivered rich and inspiring messages. In that same year, three books came from his busy pen. How wonderful that at that age, though frail in body, he was still able to share with thousands around the world the garnered fruit of his spiritual maturity.

BEREAVEMENT

As the years march on, the sorrow of the loss of loved ones becomes more and more the lot of those of us who are aging. The manner in which we handle bereavement and sorrow is a searching test of our maturity.

In writing to Miss Amy W. Carmichael of the Dohnavur Fellowship in India, Bishop Frank Houghton displayed a mature attitude about the death of his younger sister, an attitude that merits our emulation. He wrote:

> Many of our friends, in their letters of sympathy, speak of God's mysterious ways, and I know there is an element of mystery. But I shrink from the suggestion that our Father has done anything that needs to be explained. What He has done is the best, because He has done it, and I pray that as a family we may not cast about for explanation, but exult in the Holy Spirit and say, "I thank thee, Father . . . Even so, Father . . ."
>
> It suggests a lack of confidence in Him if we find it necessary to understand all He does.
>
> Will it not bring greater joy to tell Him that we need no explanation because we know Him? "As for God, his way is perfect," said the psalmist. If His way is perfect, we need no explanation.[3]

NOTES

1. Olive Wyon, *Emma Piechynska* (London: Hodder & Stoughton).
2. Arnold J. Toynbee, *Experiences* (London: Oxford University Press, 1969).
3. Frank Houghton, *Amy Carmichael of Dohnavur* (London: S.P.C.K., 1952).

8

Maturity in the Prayer Life

In the same way, the Spirit helps us in our weakness. We do not know what we ought to pray, but the Spirit himself intercedes for us with groans that words cannot express. And he who searches our hearts knows the mind of the Spirit, because the Spirit intercedes for the saints in accordance with God's will. —Romans 8:26, 27

Ask and it will be given to you; seek and you will find; knock and the door will be opened to you. For everyone who asks receives; he who seeks finds; and to him who knocks, the door will be opened. —Luke 11:9, 10

Prayer holds a vastly important place in the growth and development of the Christian life. Spiritual maturity will therefore be displayed in the quality of the believer's prayer life.

Prayer is paradoxical. No other spiritual exercise is such a blending of simplicity and complexity. Although it is "the simplest form of speech that infant lips can try," it is also "the sublimest strains that reach the Majesty on high."[1] It is as appropriate to the erudite philosopher as to the little child. It can be the spontaneous thought of a moment or the attitude of a lifetime. It is an agony and an ecstasy. It is submissive and yet importunate. It can be focused on a single objective and can roam the world.

Amid this complexity and seeming contradiction, it is small wonder that even Paul, that great exponent of the art of prayer, was forced to confess, "We do not know what we ought to pray." But he was swift to add, "The Spirit helps us in our weakness" (Rom. 8:26).

In the prayers of the mature believers, *God's interests and concerns will always be paramount.* In the immature stages of the Christian life, our prayers tend to concentrate on ourselves and our interests, and our prayers consist mainly of petition. But as we grow and bring our lives increasingly under the authority of Scripture, we learn to accord God and His interests first place in our prayers.

THE PATTERN PRAYER

Christ's pattern prayer clearly establishes this priority. He had drawn His disciples aside for a quiet retreat and was praying in their presence. When He ceased, one of them said, "Lord, teach us to pray!" He responded to their request by giving them the model prayer recorded in Matthew 6:9–13.

The first half of this prayer, on which Jesus said we were to model our own prayers, is occupied totally with God and His interests—a concern for hallowing His name, for the coming of His kingdom, and for the carrying out of His will. Only then do personal petitions have a place. We should observe this priority and give worship, adoration, and thanksgiving a proportionate place in our praying.

A study of Paul's prayers will confirm this emphasis. While a few personal petitions are included in them, the bulk of his prayers are concerned with the interests of God and other people.

PRAYING WITH AUTHORITY

Authority in prayer will be another mark of a growing maturity. The Christian is engaged in spiritual warfare against unseen and intangible spiritual forces, and for such a conflict only spiritual weapons will avail. But they are available. "The weapons we fight with are not the weapons of the world. On the contrary, they have divine power to demolish strongholds" (2 Cor. 10:4).

Of these weapons, prayer is the most formidable. "Ours is not a struggle against flesh and blood, but against the authorities, against the rulers of this dark world, and against the spiritual forces of evil in the heavenly realms" (Eph. 6:12). This seems an unequal contest, and yet it is to such a conflict that we are committed.

What is the divine strategy for this campaign? The fulcrum on which it turns is our ability to pray right. It is a spiritual as well as a military maxim that the best method of offense is attack, so the plan of our Commander is that the church should constantly be attacking on all fronts. Nowhere does He envisage a church on the defensive. It is then for us to press the battle to the very gates of Hades, and we have His assurance that they will not be able to hold out against the assault (see Matt. 16:18).

It is in this context that praying with authority proves such a potent weapon. To His seventy eager disciples the Lord said, "I saw Satan fall like lightning from Heaven. I have given you authority . . . to overcome all the power of the enemy" (Luke 10:19).

The unmistakable inference was that through the exercise of their delegated authority in their own sphere of responsibility, they too would witness the overthrow of Satan. And they were not disappointed. The radiant disciples returned from their evangelistic foray exclaiming, "Lord, even the demons submit to us in your name" (Luke 10:17).

This promised authority was not withdrawn; but when the disciples lost vital faith in Christ's promise, they were powerless even to deliver a demon-possessed boy (see Matt. 17:19). They were paralyzed by their own unbelief. After His resurrection, the Lord once again affirmed their privilege: "Making use of my name"—my authority— "they shall expel demons" (Mark 16:17 WEYMOUTH).

THE SWORD OF THE SPIRIT

Another resource is available to the praying soul, "the sword of the Spirit which is the Word of God." It was with this weapon that Jesus defeated the devil in the desert temptation. Its aggressive and overcoming power is released only in response to the prayer of faith.

Our instructions are specific: "Take . . . the sword of the Spirit, which is the word of God. And pray in the Spirit on all occasions with all kinds of prayers and requests" (Eph. 6:17–18a).

Paul does not here envisage passive, restful prayer. Only strenuous, aggressive prayer based on the Word of God will avail to dislodge the enemy from his agelong citadel. Such praying releases the resources of God and brings them into play on the field of battle. Costly? Yes, but also conquering.

"Satan dreads nothing but prayer," wrote Samuel Chadwick. "His one concern is to keep saints from praying. He fears nothing from prayerless studies, prayerless work, prayerless religion. He laughs at our toil, mocks our wisdom but trembles when we pray."

> *Restraining prayer we cease to fight,*
> *Prayer makes the Christian's armor bright;*
> *And Satan trembles when he sees*
> *The weakest saint upon his knees.*
> William Cowper

Jesus used a vivid illustration of our priorities in this spiritual warfare: "How can anyone enter a strong man's house and carry off his possessions unless he first ties up the strong man? Then he can rob his house" (Matt. 12:29).

Every believer in our day can exercise this delegated authority over Satan and his hosts. Christ's triumph can become every believer's triumph. Though pitifully weak in themselves, believers occupy a strategic role in this truceless warfare.

UNANSWERED PRAYER

The mature Christian will not be restrained by what seems to be unanswered prayer. The mature believer will seek out the cause of unanswered prayer.

Someone said, "It is easy to become a fatalist in reference to unanswered prayer." It is easier to regard it as being the will of God than to deliberately search and reason out the cause. The mature Christian will adopt the latter course. Should we be less realistic and honest in our approach to this admittedly difficult problem than a merchant to an adverse balance sheet?

Perhaps our reluctance to face and analyze our failures in prayer is rooted in a mistaken solicitude for God's honor. But in reality God is more honored when we ruthlessly face our failure and diligently search for the cause than when we piously ignore it or sweep it under the rug.

The underlying reason for every unanswered prayer is that in some way we have asked wrongly. James gives one such possible reason: "When you ask, you do not receive, because *you ask with wrong motives*" (James 4:3b, italics mine).

Or could it be that we have substituted *faith in prayer* for *faith in God?* We are nowhere exhorted to have faith in prayer, but we are counseled by the highest Authority, "Have faith in God." This may sound trite, but it is more than a matter of semantics. God is the all-important factor in prayer, and He is also the actor.

When the apostles faced the problem of failure, they asked Jesus, "Why could we not . . . ?" "Because of your unbelief," was the Lord's reply (Matt. 17:19–20). An analysis of our own prayers might uncover the disconcerting truth that many of them are not the *prayer of faith* at all, only the *prayer of hope* or even of despair. When we pray, we sincerely hope that God will answer, but often we have no unshakeable confidence that He will do so.

We should recognize that God is bound to answer only the prayer of faith, and for this we have an assuring word. "I tell you, whatever you ask for in prayer, believe that you have received it, and it will be yours" (Mark 11:24). Don't think the translator has got the tenses mixed! It is we who have got our heart attitude wrong.

DELAYED OR DENIED ANSWERS

Delays or denials in the realm of prayer will not cause the mature Christian to stumble. The mature believer recognizes and rejoices in the sovereignty of God and accepts the fact that He has a valid reason for such action or inaction. The classic example of this is in Paul's reaction to his "thorn in the flesh."

Delayed answers are not necessarily denials. God's timing is more knowledgeable and accurate than ours. We are driven by our own impatience, but God will not be pressured into premature action. If the answer is delayed, God has a good reason. The delay may be the means of needed spiritual discipline. We are here to be educated. Impatience is a form of distrust in God.

Sometimes our prayers are *denied* for reasons that our

Father sees are good. Perhaps if the precise prayer were answered, it might have undesirable side effects that we cannot see. Or it may be that God plans to give a larger answer or a higher blessing. As we get to know Him better, we are able to trust His love and wisdom even if we cannot understand His actions.

> *Unanswered yet? Though when you first presented*
> *This one petition at the Father's throne,*
> *It seemed you could not wait the time of asking,*
> *So urgent was your heart to make it known.*
> *Though years have passed since then, do not despair,*
> *The Lord will answer you*
> *Sometime, somewhere.*
>
> *Unanswered yet? Nay, do not say ungranted,*
> *Perhaps your part is not yet fully done.*
> *The work began when first your prayer was uttered,*
> *And God will finish what He has begun;*
> *If you will keep the incense burning there,*
> *His glory you will see*
> *Sometime, somewhere.*
> Ophelia R. Browning, "Unanswered Yet?"

AUDACIOUS PRAYING

The mature Christian will be no stranger to audacious praying. In the light of the wide-spreading promises made to the Intercessor, how tepid and insipid are many of our prayers! Seldom do our petitions soar above the level of natural thought or previous experience. We confine our praying to respectable requests for a minimum expenditure of divine power. How often do we dare to pray for the unprecedented, let alone the impossible?

The whole atmosphere of this materialistic age in which we live tends to make us minimize what we can expect of God; and yet Scripture encourages us to believe that the extent of legitimate expectation is literally without limits. This belief gave rise to William Carey's great motto: "Expect great things from God. Attempt great things for God."

As if to anticipate and overcome our reluctance to pray audaciously, God uses in His promises to the praying soul every universal term: whoever, whatever, whenever, all, any, every.

Take one such promise: "I tell you the truth, my Father will give you *whatever* you ask in my name" (John 16:23, italics mine). Trace the other universal terms as used in relation to prayer, and note how they encourage us to bring large petitions.

> *Come, my soul, thy suit prepare,*
> *Jesus loves to answer prayer;*
> *He Himself hath bid thee pray,*
> *Therefore will not say thee nay.*
>
> *Thou art coming to a King,*
> *Large petitions with thee bring,*
> *For his grace and power are such*
> *None can ever ask too much.*
>
> John Newton

It has been said that God's only limitation is in the character of the one who prays. Christ's affirmation, "according to your faith it will be to you," would support this contention (Matt. 9:29).

God delights to hear and answer daring prayers that are based on scriptural promises and assurances. How quickly he responded to the faith of the Syrophenician woman, even though her prayer had no right of claim (see Mark 7:24–30). Even so, Christ encourages us to ask as freely for the impossible as for the possible, since to Him all difficulties are exactly the same size—less than Himself.

It was this confidence that led Jesus to make this

astounding statement to His disciples: "I tell you the truth, if you have faith as small as a mustard seed, you can say to this mountain, 'Move from here to there,' and it will move. Nothing will be impossible for you" (Matt. 17:20).

On another occasion Christ used the illustration of a tree and not a mountain (Matt. 21:21). But audacious praying is no more dismayed by a mountain than by a tree, since "everything is possible for him who believes" (Mark 9:23).

> *'Twas most impossible of all*
> *That here in me sin's reign should cease;*
> *Yet, shall it be? I know it shall!*
> *'Tis certain though impossible!*
> *The thing impossible shall be,*
> *All things are possible to me.*
>
> Charles Wesley

WRESTLING IN PRAYER

One kind of praying is experienced only by the mature. Epaphras engaged in this type of intercession, and of him Paul wrote, "Epaphras, who is one of you and a servant of Christ Jesus . . . is always wrestling in prayer for you . . ." (Col. 4:12).

J. H. Jowett said that all vital praying makes a drain on a person's vitality. Our Lord prayed "with strong crying and tears." Our English word "agonize" is derived from the Greek word here translated "wrestling." How pale a reflection of Epaphras's wrestling are our languid prayers!

An indication of the strenuousness of this kind of praying is reflected in the fact that the same word is used of a person toiling at work until utterly weary (see Col. 1:29) and an athlete striving in the arena for the coveted prize (see 1 Cor. 9:25). It describes the soldier battling for his very life (see 1 Tim. 6:12) and the man who struggles to defend a friend from danger (see John 18:36). The whole picture is one of intense involvement, and it was thus that Paul prayed. What examples for our emulation are to be seen in the prayers of Paul and Epaphras!

THE PRAYER OF FAITH

I have previously referred to the prayer of faith. In prayer, as in every other aspect of the Christian life, there is no substitute for faith. "Without faith it is impossible to please God" (Heb. 11:6a).

The prayer of faith finds its warrant in the promises and affirmations of God in His Word, applied to our hearts by the Holy Spirit. It is a divinely given intuition and assurance that God has answered our prayer and granted our requests. It is not the outcome of our trying to believe, but it is an effortless confidence in God.

But how can one distinguish between mere natural desires and the promptings of the Holy Spirit? John comes to our assistance at this point. "This is the assurance we have in approaching God: that if we ask anything according to his will, he hears us. And if we know that he hears us— whatever we ask—*we know that we have what we asked of him*" (1 John 5:14–15, italics mine).

We must first satisfy ourselves that our petition is in harmony with the will and Word of God. Once we are sure of this, we know that He hears us because we believe He is true to His plighted Word. That being so, John says we know that we have—not will have in the future, but have obtained now—our request.

The actual enjoyment of the prayed-for blessing may be in the future, but faith regards it as already in possession. Mark 11:24 adds further confirmation: "Therefore I tell you, whatever you ask for in prayer, believe that you have received it, and it will be yours." Note, however, that it will be impossible to pray the prayer of faith for anything that is outside the scope of the will of God.

The praying Christian can believe for all that is sanctioned by the Word of God and witnessed to by His Spirit. It is in the atmosphere of prayer that the Holy Spirit nourishes and develops our faith and enables us to believe. On the other hand, it is also through prayer that the Holy Spirit indicates to us that what we desire is not God's will for us.

A CLASSIC EXAMPLE

A classic example of the prayer of faith is recounted in *The Diary of George Müller*. He writes:

> This is perhaps of all days the most remarkable so far as regards funds. When I was in prayer this morning respecting them, *I was enabled firmly to believe* that the Lord would send help, though all seemed dark as to natural appearances. At twelve o'clock I met as usual with the brethren and sisters in prayer. There had come in only one shilling, which, except twopence, had already been spent because of the great need. . . .
>
> Neither in the Infants' nor Boys' Orphan houses was there bread enough for tea, nor money to buy milk. Lower we had never been, perhaps never so low. We gave ourselves unitedly to prayer, laying the case in simplicity before the Lord. We continued for a while silently in prayer.
>
> At last we rose from our knees. I said, "God will surely send help." The words had not quite passed my lips when I saw a letter lying on the table which had been brought in while we were in prayer. It was from my wife containing another letter, which contained 10 pounds for the orphans. The prayer of faith had its reward.[2]

NOTES

1. By James Montgomery (1771–1845) in his hymn "Prayer Is the Soul's Sincere Desire."
2. A. Rendle Short, ed., *The Diary of George Müller* (Grand Rapids, Michigan: Zondervan Publishing House, 1972), p. 72.

9

Maturity Through Temptation and Testing

No temptation has seized you except what is common to man. And God is faithful; he will not let you be tempted beyond what you can bear. But when you are tempted, he will also provide a way out so that you can stand up under it. —1 Corinthians 10:13

Temptation is the uniform experience of life. "No one is so good that he is immune to temptation," wrote Thomas à Kempis. "We will never be entirely free from it. . . . There is no order so holy, no place so secret where there be no temptations."[1]

Since the Christian lives in a constant environment of temptation, no treatment of the subject of spiritual maturity would be complete without taking this into account. The mature believer is one who has learned how to meet temptation and emerge victorious.

The word "temptation" is derived from the Latin *temptare,* which bears the meaning, "to prove by trial, to put to the test." It was not until much later that the current meaning, "to entice" became common English usage.

There are two Greek words and two Hebrew words that are almost parallel in meaning, bearing on the subject of temptation.

The first two mean "to test, to assay," as when metal is tested in a crucible to separate the pure metal from the dross. These words are rarely, if ever, used in a bad sense.

They denote tests and trials sent from God. (The Hebrew word is used in Proverbs 17:3 and 1 Chronicles 29:17. The Greek word occurs in 1 Corinthians 3:13 and 1 Peter 1:7.) Although the test itself may be severe, its object is to detect alloy, not to prove the metal impure.

The second two words suggest the idea of "probing to discover the weak spots." They may be used by either friend or foe, from either good or bad motives. The Hebrew word is used of testing God in Exodus 17:7. The Greek word conveys the idea of putting someone to the test to see what good or evil is in the one tested. It gradually came to mean "solicitation or enticement to evil." Both meanings are present in Hebrews 2:18, "Because he himself suffered when he was tempted, he is able to help those who are tempted."

Testing and temptation may come from either God or Satan. God tests. The devil tempts. God never tempts man to sin. "God cannot be tempted by evil, nor does he tempt anyone" (James 1:13). Any tests He allows always have our highest interests in view. Satan tempts in order to achieve our downfall and ruin. The temptation of our Lord in the desert combined both test and temptation.

AVENUES OF TEMPTATION

Teachers in the "old school" used to say that there are three stages in every sin: the suggestion, the delectation, and the consent. Sin does not begin with the suggestion; sin begins only when the suggestion is entertained and acted on.

It is significant that the same three elements appeared both in the temptation of the first Adam in Eden and in that of the second Adam in the desert.

A study of the three temptations of Christ indicates that they were representative temptations that cover the whole range of human desire. When the author of the Book of Hebrews wrote, "We have a high priest who has been tempted in every way, just as we are," he did not mean that Jesus experienced every specific temptation that men and women have suffered through the ages. For example, how could He have suffered the peculiar temptations of the space age?

The meaning is that temptation assailed Him along every avenue in which it can reach our human nature. The surrounding circumstances and incidentals may vary greatly, but in essence, temptations are basically the same for all men and women in all ages.

It has been suggested that temptation assails us along three main avenues, and all other temptations are only variants of these.

The first is *appetite, the desire to enjoy things*. John terms this "the cravings of the sinful man" (1 John 2:16). Satan made his first approach to Jesus on the *physical* plane (see Matt. 4:2–3). He stirred up a natural and legitimate desire, but he pressured the Lord to go beyond the bounds set by God. The focus of the temptation was not on Christ's right to satisfy His hunger, but on His submission to the will of God. To have yielded to Satan's lure would have meant satisfying a legitimate craving in an illegitimate way. Satan was foiled in this attempt.

The second is *ambition, the desire to achieve great things, to be somebody* (see Matt. 4:5–6). This, John designates "boasting of what he has and does" (1 John 2:16). The devil's second approach to Jesus was on the *mental* plane. It focused on our Lord's confidence in His Father. Satan challenged Christ to demonstrate His faith by putting His Father's promise to the test; but Jesus replied that for Him to do so would be presumption, not faith. Once again He refused to go beyond the limits God had laid down for Him.

The third avenue through which temptation can reach

man is *avarice, the desire to get possession of things* (see Matt. 4:8–11). John terms this "the lust of his eyes" (1 John 2:16). Avarice is yielding to the temptation to put things in the place of God. Satan demanded that Jesus accord him the place that belongs to God alone. The focus of this temptation was on the possibility that Christ could achieve His purpose and obtain His kingdom without the anguish and agony of the Cross.

Once again the Lord unsheathed the sword of the Spirit and routed the tempter. Having failed in his attempt to storm the citadel of Christ's loyalty and obedience to His Father, the devil left Him, but only "for a season."

It is along these three avenues—appetite (hunger, thirst, and sex), ambition (the craving for position and power), and avarice (the passion to accumulate possessions)—that temptations come to people today as well. But when our Lord overcame Satan on all three points, He made it possible for us to overcome in these areas too.

> *For us baptized, for us He bore*
> *His holy fast and hungered sore;*
> *For us temptations sharp He knew,*
> *For us the tempter overthrew.*
>
> *Cold mountains and the midnight air*
> *Witnessed the fervour of Thy prayer;*
> *The desert Thy temptations knew,*
> *Thy conflict and Thy victory too.*
>
> Anonymous

BLESSING THROUGH TEMPTATION

"No Christian, however ripe their experience, however established in character, however fruitful in service will ever get beyond the possibility of backsliding."

These solemn warning words do not overstate the fact.

Since we will be tempted until our dying day, Christianity must be able to provide the answer to daily temptation in every form. And it does.

Temptations are often a blessing in disguise. As Thomas à Kempis put it, "Temptation can be a service to us. It may be a burden, but it can bring us humility and teach us good lessons. All of the saints experienced more than their share of trials and temptations, and they grew as a result."[2] God uses Satan for purposes of sanctification.

Sir Isaac Newton once said that trials are medicines that our wise Physician prescribes because we need them. And He prescribes the amount and the correct proportion that the case requires. All our temptations are adjusted by God. They will never be so long or so fierce as to preclude the possibility of victory.

The passage at the head of this chapter is the classic Scripture statement about temptation, and it is preceded by the warning: "If you think that you are standing firm, be careful that you don't fall!" (1 Cor. 10:12). It assures that there is a way out of temptation as well as a way into it. The key of victory is hanging near the door. It is our responsibility to use it. The way of escape is always the same—the trusted Christ.

> *Tempted and tried!*
> *O the terrible tide*
> *May be raging and deep,*
> *May be wrathful and wide;*
> *Yet its fury is vain*
> *For the Lord shall restrain,*
> *And for ever and ever*
> *Jehovah shall reign.*
>
> Frances R. Havergal

GOD'S VOTE OF CONFIDENCE

God expresses His confidence that His trusting children will be able to survive the test. His faithfulness to His Word is stressed before the assurance that He will not allow us to be tempted beyond our capacity to survive the temptation. With this confidence, it is for us to quietly trust Him to keep His Word. He will never allow His children to come to a place where sin is inevitable, for sin is not a fatalistic necessity to the believer.

> *Tempted and tried!*
> *There is One at thy side,*
> *And never in vain*
> *Shall His children confide,*
> *He shall save and defend*
> *For he loves to the end.*
> *Adorable Master*
> *And glorious Friend.*
>
> Frances R. Havergal

THE INCIDENCE OF TEMPTATION

We can gain insight into our adversary's methods from a study of our Lord's representative temptations.

The trials came after a time of rich blessing. At Christ's baptism and the descent of the Spirit, His Father had expressed His unbounded approval of His Son (see Matt. 3:17). *"Then* was Jesus led by the Spirit into the desert to be tempted by the devil" (Matt. 4:1). After the Dove, the devil. After the blessing, the battle. This is often the sequence, and it has been so down the ages.

The trials came in an inhospitable environment—the desert. The fact that we have experienced a time of great blessing does not alter the reality of returning to face difficult conditions. Indeed, our circumstances may change for the worse. We can take courage from the fact that Jesus proved His Father's care even in the loneliness of the barren desert.

The trials came when Christ's body was weak through fasting. It is easier to meet temptation when we are in top physical form, but the devil is a dirty fighter. He delights to launch his fiery darts when we are weary and under pressure. The laws of nature still apply even though we are engaged in the Lord's service, and we should be careful to guard against a reckless overexpenditure of physical and nervous energy.

Some temptations come unsought and in the ordinary course of our vocation. For these we cannot attach blame. We voluntarily walk into other temptations by yielding to wrong impulses. These are blameworthy. Joseph was an example of the first, David of the second.

JOSEPH'S TEMPTATION AND VICTORY

Joseph's critical test and temptation came entirely unexpectedly and in the course of his ordinary duties as Potiphar's steward. On entering the house on one occasion the wife of Joseph's master tried to seduce him (see Gen. 39). The circumstances made it very easy for capitulation but terribly difficult for the triumph of virtue.

Everything favored capitulation. Satan had chosen the optimum moment to stage his assault. Joseph was living away from home and was desperately lonely. He was living in a wicked and licentious society. The temptation gained power from its unexpectedness. It came at a moment when his influence with his master was at its zenith. It would be in his interests to stand well with his master's wife.

Joseph had no time to brace himself for the shock—temptation does not wait for us to don our armor before it strikes. If we wait until temptation comes before deciding how we will act, we have waited too long. It is as unpredictable as lightning. It is not difficult to imagine the tumult of emotions in a young man of twenty-seven years, at the height of his virility.

As if these factors were not sufficient, the temptation was renewed day after day. A single, sudden temptation is one thing. But when it recurs every day, that is quite another. Many who resist at first succumb at last. Persistence often wears down resistance.

But Joseph emerged from this stupendous test with his virtue unsullied because he refused to entertain for even a moment any suggestion that would induce him to sin against his God. "How could I do such a wicked thing and sin against God?" he said to his temptress.

The devil selects the most auspicious occasion to strike! "None of the household servants was inside" (Gen. 39:11). Joseph's safety lay in his desire to stand well in the sight of God rather than in the eyes of his master's wife. This proved a bulwark amid the storm that raged within. God's people are always motivated by principle, not by expediency. Joseph had to pay a high price for his purity, but in the end he received magnificent recompense.

From this classic example of temptation issuing in triumph, we can learn several lessons, especially about sexual sin. First, temptation itself is not sin, for Jesus was tempted, and He did not sin. Temptation becomes sin only when entertained and yielded to. Second, sexual desire in itself is not wrong. Third, legitimate desire may be satisfied from illegitimate sources, and this constitutes sin.

In the interests of the individual and of society as a whole, God has fixed clearly defined bounds in this area. To transgress them incurs guilt and penalty. To voluntarily walk into such temptation is to forfeit any claim to divine help. Because Joseph's test came in the course of duty, he could claim and expect God's help in the hour of need.

As in Joseph's case, flight is sometimes the only safe

course. Joseph gained his final victory by taking to his heels, regardless of the consequences, and thus he escaped from the zone of temptation. The lesson is that we must kill the serpent, not stroke it.

DAVID'S TEMPTATION

How different was the case of King David when he was confronted with a similar temptation. In David's case the temptation resulted in ruinous defeat. The solemn aspect of the story is recorded in 2 Samuel 11.

If, as his psalms would lead us to believe, David was a true man of God, how can we explain the stark contrasts between Joseph's reactions and David's reactions to the same temptation? The answer is in part that, in contrast to Joseph, *David was conditioned to fall.* In instructing Israel about the conduct of the king they would have, God had said, "He must not take many wives or his heart will be led astray" (Deut. 17:17). David had disobeyed and taken many wives. Thus he was weakened by his previous indulgence.

David's fall occurred at a time of abounding success and prosperity, when one is less likely to be strongly disciplined. Prosperity is not sin, but it is always a stringent test. David's temptation happened at a time of indolence and sloth, after an unduly prolonged siesta. It was "at the time when kings go off to war." Had David not neglected his responsibilities as king, the temptation would not have arisen.

David could doubtless rationalize his remaining at home. Had he not earned the right to take some relaxation? Could not the king walk on his roof and enjoy the beauty of the gardens around, if he chose? In this state of weakness and indulgence, David's fatal temptation met him in the form of a beautiful woman.

Joseph triumphed where David succumbed because he was walking in fellowship with God and in the line of duty. David fell because he was out of touch with God and was neglecting his kingly duties. True, David experienced a momentary gratification, but his actions brought life-long remorse and family tragedy in its train. The sequel in the lives of these two men provides overwhelming evidence that virtue and godliness pay handsome and tangible dividends even here and now; but sin pays bitter wages.

Joseph was a young man who displayed unusual maturity in his attitude to temptation, and he provides a model for succeeding generations. David was an old and mature saint whose fall warns that spiritual maturity is not synonymous with age and can be forfeited through sin.

"Some people retreat from difficulties or deny they exist," wrote Charles Sell. "Many are ashamed of their struggles, because of the prevalent attitude that the Christian life should be problem-free. . . . We confuse being saved from sin with being saved from struggle. But faith does not spare us from the battle; it prepares us to face it."[3]

NOTES

1. As quoted in Bernard Bangley, *Growing in His Image* (Wheaton, Illinois: Harold Shaw Publishers, 1983), p. 35.
2. Ibid.
3. Charles Sell, "How to Faith It," *Moody Monthly* (March, 1978), p. 40.

10

Mature Reactions to Circumstances

I rejoice greatly in the Lord that at last you have renewed your concern for me. Indeed, you have been concerned, but you had no opportunity to show it. I am not saying this because I am in need, for I have learned to be content whatever the circumstances. *I know what it is to be in need, and I know what it is to have plenty.* I have learned the secret of being content in any and every situation, *whether well fed or hungry, whether living in plenty or in want. I can do everything through him who gives me strength.* —Philippians 4:10–13, emphasis added

Paul, who penned these amazing words, demonstrated that he had reached an advanced stage of spiritual maturity. For our comfort it should be noted that he did not claim, "I have *always* been content whatever the circumstances," but "I have *learned* the secret of being content." The lessons doubtless had continued over a considerable period, but the encouraging point is that he had learned and mastered the secret.

If Paul could learn contentment, so can we. God has no favorites, and Paul had no resources that are not available to us. One need review only a few of the adverse circumstances cataloged in 2 Corinthians 11:23–29, over which Paul emerged victorious, to appreciate the magnitude of his triumph.

Are they servants of Christ? . . . I am more . . . I have worked much harder, been in prison more frequently, been flogged more severely, and been exposed to death again and again. Five times I received from the Jews the forty lashes minus one. Three times I was beaten with rods, once I was stoned, three times I was shipwrecked. —2 Corinthians 11:23–25

These are only a selection of his sufferings. In Romans 8:35–37 he lists seven of the worst conceivable circumstances we could encounter—trouble, hardship, persecution, famine, nakedness, danger, sword—and then he adds the triumphant conclusion: "In all these things we are *more than conquerors* through him who loved us" (Rom. 8:37, italics mine). How small and trifling do our difficult circumstances seem when compared with what Paul endured; and yet so often they conquer us and get us down. Let us remind ourselves that we can draw on the same resources that Paul appropriated, and in our measure we can rise above our distresses as he did.

MATURITY REVEALED IN REACTIONS

Our maturity is most accurately reflected in our attitudes and unstudied reactions to our circumstances, especially the unwelcome and unexpected ones. Paul's maturity shone brightly in his reactions to his unjust imprisonments. In the inner prison in Philippi, with their feet in the cruel stocks, he and Silas sang songs in the night.

When later Paul was imprisoned again and wrote his letter to the Philippians, far from bemoaning his circumstances, his theme song was, "Rejoice in the Lord always. I will say it again: Rejoice!" (Phil. 4:4). He drew strength and courage from the knowledge that God was still on His throne and he was safe in his Father's hands.

The word "learned" that Paul used is the normal word for learning at school. The child learns by adding new knowledge to what he or she has already learned. The disciple has to learn in exactly the same way. Even the Son of God could not go through life wearing our humanity without submitting to the learning process. "Although he was a son, he learned obedience from what he suffered" (Heb. 5:8). And the result? "Once made perfect [mature], he became the source of eternal salvation for all who obey him" (Heb. 5:9).

It is for us who desire to grow in maturity to place ourselves under the skillful tutelage of the Divine Teacher and diligently endeavor to master the lessons He sees we need to learn.

Paul's attitude was not that of the fatalist or of the stoic who bows to the inevitable. Rather it was the attitude of glad acceptance. "For Christ's sake I delight in weaknesses, in insults, in difficulties"—the very things we would give anything to avoid. Then he shared his secret— "For when I am weak, then I am strong" (2 Cor. 12:10b).

The reader's reaction to the foregoing may very well be, "But that was Paul, the greatly gifted apostle. I am no Paul. Such lofty heights are far above the possible level of my attainment." But the fact is that very many ordinary people have experienced the same triumphs through mastering Paul's secret.

TRIUMPH OVER CIRCUMSTANCES

It is all too possible that even after we have gained victory over besetting sins, we are laid low by our circumstances—illness, bereavement, anxiety, financial reverses, advancing old age, marital and family problems, or physical weakness.

It would be unrealistic to deny the poignancy of the

suffering that such circumstances generate. But biblical history and the experience of a host of contemporary Christians demonstrate how frail and fallible men and women like ourselves have been able to soar above their imprisoning circumstances.

While we genuinely desire to grow in the knowledge of God, most of us insist on drawing up our own syllabus of studies. We want to dictate our own curriculum. But our kind and all-wise Father will not pander to our weak desirings. He loves us too well to allow us to cheat ourselves out of His highest and best blessings.

"God could have kept the three young men—Shadrach, Meshach and Abednego—out of the fiery furnace," wrote Ruth Paxson, "but instead He permitted them to be in there with it heated seven times hotter than usual. But what did it do? It burned off their fetters! Do we want our fetters to go? 'O, yes!' we cry, 'but not in the fiery furnace. Let them somehow be burned off outside! We don't want it that much.' "[1]

Yet it was in the searing flames of the furnace that the Lord came down and walked with His three loyal servants. If we really want to get to know God in more than a superficial way, we should take careful note that the new revelation of God came to them *inside* the fiery furnace. Nor will we experience it outside it.

> He placed thee 'midst this dance
> Of plastic circumstance,
> Machinery just meant
> To give thy soul its bent.
>
> Robert Browning

DISCIPLINE IS NOT PLEASANT

In their usual realistic style, the biblical writers do not glamorize the discipline process. "No discipline seems pleasant at the time, but painful. Later on, however, it produces a harvest of righteousness and peace for those who have been trained by it" (Heb. 12:11). We would all covet the "later on" experience, if only what went before could be eliminated or ameliorated. But it cannot be so.

We would like to know the power of God resting on us and our service, but not at the cost of suffering some limiting handicap. Yet Paul arrived at the place where he could actually boast and rejoice in his weaknesses in order that the power of Christ might rest on him. How did he reach that place? By accepting without a grumble the painful "thorn in the flesh," which God gave him to keep him from being too conceited (2 Cor. 12:7–10). Paul did not say that he *enjoyed* it, but he *rejoiced* in it. He was content with weakness if it meant experiencing more of the power of Christ.

ATTITUDE TO CIRCUMSTANCES

Most of us shine better when we come out of difficult and distressing circumstances. Paul shone more brightly while he was in the midst of them. Wherein lay his secret?

Acceptance, not rebellion

Anyone can resist or rebel against God, and charge Him with not treating them fairly. "Why should this happen to me?" we protest. The mature Christian accepts the biblical teaching that nothing happens apart from divine permission, even though the reason may not be immediately apparent. This attitude enables the mature believer to discern that the will of God is indeed good and acceptable and perfect.

Contentment, not complaining.

Anyone can complain at what God allows. Only the mature Christian knows contentment in the midst of it. As a nation, the Hebrews were continual complainers, a quality that marred their history. The same quality is evident in many immature believers today. In church and home they are usually the ones who complain or are at the center of dissension.

In one area of Mexico women can wash their clothes in hot and cold springs that are very close to each other. While watching the women one day, a tourist remarked to his guide, "I suppose the women think Mother Nature is very good to them."

"No, exactly the opposite," was the rejoinder. "There is much grumbling, because there is no soap!"

The growing Christian heeds the injunction, "Be content with what you have" (Heb. 13:5) and proves in experience that "godliness with contentment is great gain" (1 Tim. 6:6). The mature believer assents to the fact that if God's will is "perfect," it cannot be improved on, and therefore he or she can be content.

Trustfulness, not anxiety

The natural reaction to difficult or threatening circumstances is to indulge in an orgy of worry and anxiety. I used to have on the wall of my office a motto that said, *"Why pray when you can worry?"* Many visitors who read it thought there had been a mistake in the wording. But I would point out to them that the motto reflected only too accurately the attitude of many Christians who found themselves in trying circumstances.

Have we not often proved that the calamity we foresaw and worried about never came to pass? And yet we continue our ulcer-producing, peace-destroying habit of worrying. Our Lord's homily on "anxiety" in the Sermon on the Mount emphasized that worry is needless, futile, and faithless. Worse than that, it is pagan (Matt. 6:32).

Hudson Taylor of China affirmed that "there should be only one circumstance to us in life, and that circumstance is GOD." Anxiety stems from the lack of quiet trust and confidence in our loving an omnipotent God.

NOTES

1. From a pamphlet by Ruth Paxson.

11

The Maturing Fire of the Spirit

In that day the Branch of the Lord will be beautiful and glorious, and the fruit of the land will be the pride and glory of the survivors in Israel. . . . The Lord will wash away the filth of the women of Zion; he will cleanse the bloodstains from Jerusalem by a spirit of judgment and a spirit of fire. Then the Lord will create over all of Mount Zion and over those who assemble there a cloud of smoke by day and a glow of flaming fire by night; over all the glory will be a canopy. —Isaiah 4:2, 4–5

In this optimistic chapter, the prophet Isaiah envisions a day when the remaining inhabitants of Jerusalem would be beautiful and glorious, clean and holy, a day when all filth and defilement would be purged away. The agent in this cleansing process, he calls the "Spirit of judgment" and the "Spirit of fire."

Since Scripture so frequently uses the symbol of fire to represent the Holy Spirit, it is not straining the text to see here a reference to His activity. As the spirit of judgment, He convicts the conscience of sin and defilement. As the spirit of fire, or "burning" (RSV), He deals with and consumes the revealed impurities. The concept of burning by a spirit is obviously allegorical, but it is explained by the New Testament.

Of all natural forces, fire is the most terrible and awe-inspiring. People of all religions and races in all ages have held it in superstitious awe. The Parsees of India still worship fire with fanatical veneration.

The symbol occurs four hundred times in the Old Testament and seventy-five times in the New, and almost all are linked with the presence and power of God as a living flame. Just as the sun is the source of power in the terrestrial realm, so is the Holy Spirit in the spiritual realm. Hymnology is replete with such references:

> *Come, Thou burning Spirit, come,*
>   *Lo! we stretch our hands to Thee;*
> *From the Father to the Son,*
>   *Let us now Thy glory see.*
>
> Caroline Fry

> *Refining fire go through my heart,*
>   *Illuminate my soul;*
> *Scatter Thy light through every part*
>   *And sanctify the whole.*
>
> Charles Wesley

> *O Thou who camest from above*
>   *The pure, celestial fire to impart,*
> *Kindle a fire of sacred love*
>   *On the mean altar of my heart.*
>
> Charles Wesley

John the Baptist announced to those who were coming to him for baptism, "I baptize you with water for repentance. But after me will come one who is more powerful than I, whose sandals I am not fit to carry. He will baptize you with the Holy Spirit and with fire" (Matt 3:11). In this passage he is not implying that the fire is a separate agency, different from the Holy Spirit, but he is rather describing the Spirit's powerful purifying influence.

So it is in keeping with the tenor of Scripture to see in the symbol of fire the activity of the Holy Spirit as the spirit of fire, of burning. When Isaiah's prophecy had its fulfillment on the Day of Pentecost, the fire was not punitive, but purifying just as the burning coal of fire purified Isaiah's own lips (see Isaiah 6:6–7).

The maturing function of fire is illustrated in three processes described in Scripture, each of which contributes to the rounding out of Christian character.

THE CONSUMING FIRE OF THE FARMER

> He will baptize you with the Holy Spirit and with fire. His winnowing fork is in his hand, and he will clear his threshing floor, gathering the wheat into his barn and burning up the chaff with unquenchable fire.
> —Matthew 3:11b–12

The significance of John the Baptist's statement would be quickly grasped by his hearers who constantly observed the threshing process. They may well have been looking at a farmer doing what John had described at that very moment. The threshing floor was usually set in a windswept area. The farmer would lift the grain with a large wooden fork, called a fan, and would toss it into the air time and again until the light chaff and straw was blown away, while the heavy grain would fall to the ground. The grain was stored in the barn, and the chaff was burned. This is what is meant by "he will clear his threshing floor." The purpose of the operation was to conserve the valuable and to consume the useless.

The winnowing freed the grain from all that would diminish its value or hinder its usefulness as food. The husk, which had once been absolutely essential to its development, had now become a liability. Its function had been completed. Now it must be separated from the grain and burnt, or it might drift back and spoil the grain's quality.

In all our lives there is the good and precious that comes from God as well as the evil that comes from the devil or from our own perverse hearts. The aids and comforters that are appropriate to spiritual infancy are not appropriate to maturity, and they actually become a hindrance. To effect a separation of the valuable from the useless, the agency used is the fiery ministry of the Holy Spirit whom Isaiah calls "the spirit of burning." The useless must be removed in the interests of maturity.

Was this not, in part what happened on the Day of Pentecost? The Spirit consumed the disciples' craven fear and made them as bold as lions. The Spirit incinerated their unbelief and made them "full of faith and of the Holy Spirit," The Spirit burned up their self-seeking and instead kindled in their hearts a leaping flame of selfless love.

> O that in me the sacred fire
> Might now begin to glow,
> Burn up the dross of base desire
> And make the mountains flow.
>> Charles Wesley

The expression "burning up the chaff with unquenchable fire" seems to smack of ruthlessness. But are not some sins so deeply entrenched that only some such drastic and radical treatment will avail to cleanse heart and life? The Heavenly Farmer loves us too well to allow us to cling to our infantile comforters, so He allows the fires of affliction to do their work—but always under the sympathetic supervision of the Holy Spirit.

Is there still chaff and straw on the floor of our lives that needs to be consumed?

THE PURIFYING FIRE OF THE REFINER

"See, I will send my messenger, who will prepare the way before me. Then suddenly the Lord you are seeking will come to his temple; the messenger of the covenant, whom you desire, will come," says the Lord Almighty. "But who can endure the day of his coming? Who can stand when he appears? For he will be like a refiner's fire or a launderer's soap. He will sit as a refiner and purifier of silver; he will purify the Levites and refine them like gold and silver. Then the Lord will have men who will bring offerings in righteousness." —Malachi 3:1–3

"I will turn my hand against you; I will thoroughly purge away your dross and remove your impurities." —Isaiah 1:25

Two purifying agents—fire and soap—are recognized in this passage.The *external* impurities clinging to the gold or silver ore can be removed by the application of soap and water, but only fire can reach and remove the *internal,* hidden impurities—dross, slag, alloy—embedded in the ore.

So the externals of religion may remove surface stains from our lives and make us outwardly presentable, but they are powerless to effect any cleansing of the inner impurities embedded in the subconscious. Our Lord left us in no doubt of the foul brood inherent in every heart: "Out of men's hearts come evil thoughts, sexual immorality, theft, murder, adultery, greed, malice, deceit, lewdness, envy, slander, arrogance, and folly" (Mark 7:21–22). Only the fire of the Holy Spirit can penetrate these hidden depths. Only He can effectively deal with such deep seated habits and ingrained sins.

The refining process is simple, but it demands considerable expertise. The refiner places the gold in the crucible that is suspended over a fierce flame. As the gold melts, the impurities are released and rise to the surface. The refiner removes the worthless scum that would diminish the value of the gold. Only when the refiner can see his own undimmed likeness reflected in the molten metal is the purifying process complete.

Unfortunately, some Christians never experience this deep inner cleansing of the Holy Spirit and are content with the superficial application of soap and water that will make them outwardly presentable. The deepest ills of the human heart are beyond the skill of the psychiatrist.

When we find ourselves in the crucible, we can take comfort in the fact that it is only because the Refiner desires to remove everything that will prevent us from reaching full maturity. The fire cannot touch our essential personality but will destroy only the useless and harmful. The fire of the Spirit can achieve the impossible, as it did on Mount Carmel (see 1 Kings 18:38). It will purge our hearts not only from disreputable sins, but also from "respectable" sins such as pride, envy, jealousy, criticism, and unforgiveness. In their place He will substitute His own fruit (see Gal. 5:22–23).

"How long will I have to remain in this crucible?" is the cry of the tested saint. Dr. A. T. Pierson gives the answer:

> Our Father who seeks to perfect His saints in holiness knows the value of the refiner's fire. It is with the most precious metals that the assayer takes the most pains, and subjects them to the hot fire, because such fires melt the metal, and only the molten mass releases its alloy and takes perfectly its new form in the mold.
>
> *The old refiner never leaves his crucible, but sits down by it,* lest there should be one excessive degree of heat to mar the metal. But as soon as he skims from the surface the last of the dross, and sees his own face reflected, he puts out the fire. (italics mine)

The Heavenly Refiner is kind enough not to let the fire die down until the dross is removed and His beneficent purpose achieved. As Pierson says, "The very fact of trial proves that there is something in us very precious to our

Lord, else He would not spend so much pain and time on us. Christ would not test us if He did not see the precious ore of faith mingled in the rocky matrix of our nature; and it is to bring out this purity and beauty that He forces us through the fiery ordeal."

The objective of the farmer was to conserve the pure grain. The purpose of the refiner is to conserve the pure gold or silver, free from all useless dross or alloy. Because these metals are incombustible, they can survive the fiercest flame and come out purified. "When he has tested me, I will come forth as gold," said the much-tried Job (Job 23:10b).

So will it be with the genuine believer. The fires of affliction and sorrow will not overwhelm but will sweeten and sanctify.

> *When through fiery trials I cause thee to go,*
> *The rivers of grief shall not thee overflow*
> *The flame shall not hurt thee, I only design*
> *Thy dross to consume and thy gold to refine.*
> George Keith

THE MATURING FIRE OF THE POTTER

This is the word that came to Jeremiah from the Lord: "Go down to the potter's house, and there I will give you my message." So I went down to the potter's house, and I saw him working at the wheel.
—Jeremiah 18:1–3

Yet, O Lord, you are our Father. We are the clay, you are the potter; we are all the work of your hand.
—Isaiah 64:8

In all eastern lands the potter is a familiar figure, with revolving wheels, malleable clay, and skillful fingers under which the clay is molded into a vessel of symmetry and beauty.

In Jeremiah's parable, the potter's fire is not mentioned, but it is an essential part of the potter's art. Without the fire, the soft clay would soon collapse and become a shapeless mass. So God subjects His children to the fires of testing lest their characters become flabby and formless. Lessons learned in the fire are not soon forgotten.

Once the potter has molded the vessel and painted on it the desired pattern, he encloses it in a fire-resistant case and places it in a furnace heated to the appropriate temperature. In the fire, moisture evaporates and unwanted materials are burned out, while the color and pattern are burned in. In this way the design and pattern are rendered permanent.

Note that the vessel does not go into the fire uncovered and unprotected. Similarly the believer is not alone in the furnace of affliction. He or she is environed by God. "When you walk through the fire, you will not be burned; the flames will not set you ablaze. For I am the Lord your God" (Isa. 43:2b–3a).

Cortland Myers writes:

> The finest china in the world is burned at least three times, some of it more than three times, Dresden china is always burned three times. Why does it go through the intense fire? Once ought to be enough. Twice ought to be enough. No, three times are necessary to burn the china so that the gold and the crimson are brought out more beautiful and then fastened there to stay.
>
> We are fashioned after the same principle in human life. Our trials are burned into us once, twice, thrice; and by God's grace these beautiful colors are there and they are there to stay forever.

It is told of King George VI of Britain that on one occasion he was taken on a tour of a pottery factory. When the party reached one room, the workman in charge directed the king's attention to a black tea set, and said,

"This is the tea set we are making for the palace, your Majesty."

"But we have not ordered a black tea set," protested the king.

"No, sir," was the answer. "But underneath the black is gold. If we put the gold into the fire unprotected it would damage the set. The fire burns off the black and reveals the gold."[1]

So often we see only the black side of the circumstances of life, but our heavenly Potter knows that the gold is underneath. We feel that our lives are so drab and ordinary, and we forget that God is directing the fire carefully in order to burn off the black and reveal the gold. Let us have patience and wait until the spirit of burning has completed His work.

> *Marred in the making, but with wondrous patience*
> *Takes He the clay*
> *Into His hands, and fashions slowly*
> *In His own way;*
> *Just what I was, the world can only see—*
> *He looks beyond, and sees what I can be.*
>
> Anonymous

NOTES

1. J. Oswald Sanders, *Christ Indwelling and Enthroned* (London: Marshall, Morgan & Scott, 1949), p. 38.

12

The Attractiveness of Maturity

But thanks be to God, who always leads us in triumphal procession in Christ and through us spreads everywhere the fragrance of the knowledge of him. For we are to God the aroma of Christ among those who are being saved and those who are perishing. To the one we are the smell of death; to the other, the fragrance of life. —2 Corinthians 2:14–16

Fragrance. Aroma. Perfume. Scent. What delightful associations and memories these words evoke! "A part of the reason for the unique place odor plays in our lives," writes Thomas D. Parks, "is the great variety of responses that the same perfume evokes when smelled by different people. In one it may bring back the memory of a vacation in childhood, in another a hike beside a mountain stream, and in still others a stroll in a garden with a lover. Thus a perfume can become a very personal and subjective experience, difficult, if not impossible to explain."[1]

A transforming experience in my life took place in my youth at Pounawea, a little seaside resort in the south of New Zealand. At Christmas the whole countryside was redolent with the strong, sweet scent of the yellow lupine. I can never smell that scent without vividly recalling the sacred experience of those days.

In his choice brochure *Fragrance Ascending*, George Armerding asserts that there is an odor of some sort associated with many of the great events of Scripture.[2] At our Lord's birth, for example, the wise men brought gifts of the fragrant frankincense and myrrh. At His death, Joseph of Arimathea brought one hundred pounds of aromatic spices with which to embalm Him.

Moved by the Holy Spirit, Paul used this lovely symbol of fragrance to illustrate the subtle power of the unconscious influence of the Christian in the midst of the corrupting influences of the world around him. Paul also used it to exemplify the joy and pleasure a fragrant life can bring, not only to a dusty, dirty world, but to the Creator Himself. "We are *to God* the aroma of Christ" (2 Cor. 2:15a, italics mine).

The imagery behind 2 Corinthians 2:14–16 is clearly that of the triumphal procession accorded to a conquering Roman general as he returns from a victorious campaign. "Thanks be to God who always leads us in triumphal procession in Christ," Paul exclaims. In that vivid pageantry he saw a graphic foreshadowing of Christ's ultimate triumph over all opposition at the consummation of the age.

Heedless of consistency as he often was, the apostle saw himself in three roles in the pageant. First, he saw himself as a vanquished prisoner, led in chains in Christ's triumphal progress. Next, he saw himself as a slave carrying a smoking censer of fragrant incense before the Victor's chariot. Finally, he conceived of himself and his colleagues as the very incense itself, as it ascended from a hundred censers along the route of the procession.

WHAT IS THIS FRAGRANCE?

Is it the fragrance of the attractive personalities of the messengers? Assuredly not. It is the winsomeness and attractiveness of Christ imparted to them by the Holy

Spirit and diffused everywhere through their preached word. "Through us spreads everywhere *the fragrance of the knowledge of him*" (2 Cor. 2:14, italics mine). The aroma of Christ pervaded their world like a cloud of fragrant incense.

> *Rich the roses' perfume, but richer far than they,*
> *The countless charms that round Thy presence play;*
> *That name alone, more fragrant than the rose,*
> *Glads everyone on whom the fragrance grows.*
>
> Anonymous

After the disciples had spent some time under the tutelage of the Lord, was it not said of them that they "took note that these men had been with Jesus"? (Acts 4:13). They exemplified the truth of Seneca's words, "He who frequents the perfumer's shop and lingers even a short time, will carry with him the scent of the place."

"It was said that excerpts from the diary of Robert Murray McCheyne are like exhalations from an eastern garden out of which flows the scent of camphor and spikenard, calamus and cinnamon, myrrh and aloes, with all the chief spices."[3]

A large group of young women who had just arrived from their homelands were beginning to learn the Chinese language in the language school of the China Inland Mission in an interior city of China. One morning the superintendent, Mrs. Alice McFarlane, entered the lecture room, walked up one aisle and down the other, and left the room without uttering a word. The girls looked at each other and wondered what it was all about. In a few minutes the superintendent returned.

"Did you notice anything when I passed through the room?" she asked.

No one volunteered a reply at first, and then one girl said, "I did notice you were wearing a fragrant perfume."

"Yes," was the reply. "Did I say anything as I walked through the room?"

"No."

"You have come to China to make Christ known to the women of this land, but you are dumb. You can't speak a word to them, and it will be a long time before you can communicate the gospel to them effectively, and you will find this frustrating. As you noticed, I did not say a word, but I did leave a sweet fragrance behind me.

"Although you may not be able to speak fluently for a long time, if you live near to the Lord, as you move in and out among these Chinese women, you can leave behind you the sweet fragrance of Christ."

THE TRIUMPHAL PROCESSION

A public procession was the highest honor a grateful nation could bestow on its victorious military leaders. Rome conferred such an honor on Titus after his gory conquest of Jerusalem in A.D. 70. At the head of his triumphal march, as tangible evidence of his boasted triumph over the Jews and their Jehovah, gleamed the golden lampstand and the Table of the Presence, which he had pillaged from the temple.

Next followed a white bull for sacrifice to the gods, and then the captured generals, leaders, and princes. Standing in a chariot drawn by four horses was the richly robed victor, accompanied by pagan priests swinging their smoking censers, impregnating the whole procession with perfume. Titus' family and the army completed the procession and filled the air with shouts of triumph as they paraded along the garlanded roads.

CHRISTIANITY, A CRUSADING RELIGION

Paul saw in this brilliant pageant a picture of Christianity as a crusading religion, with the victorious Christ at its head, marching in irresistible triumph from continent to continent and from age to age. He saw Calvary as the battleground on which Christ achieved His epochal triumph over the massed forces of evil. There "having disarmed the powers and authorities, he made a public spectacle of them, triumphing over them by the cross" (Col. 2:15).

It has not always seemed as if Christ is leading His army in triumph. But when viewed from a wider perspective, it will be seen that in every attempt the Adversary has made to achieve a decisive and final victory over the church, he has been foiled. Today Christianity is seeing greater advances and more glorious victories than ever before.

Some engagements in this age-long campaign have been lost because of the frailty of the warriors, but the victorious issue of the whole campaign is beyond doubt. He "always leads us in triumphal procession," Paul reminds us in 2 Corinthians 2:14. Christ rides in triumph, with us, His captives, willingly chained to His chariot wheel.

Paul, who gloried in the title "bondservant of Jesus Christ," saw himself also as a revolutionary leader who had ravaged the church because of the impostor Jesus but Paul had been humiliatingly defeated. One stronger than he had disarmed him, and now, chained with chains of love, he meekly follows in the train of Christ's triumph. Paul became victor through being vanquished.

THE AROMA OF CHRIST

"We are to God the aroma of Christ" (2 Cor. 2:15a). What an audacious assertion—unless it is true! We actually remind God of Christ. The figure has changed again, and Paul and his colleagues are now the fragrant perfume, the very aroma of Christ. They not only bear and diffuse the fragrance, they are the very incense itself. "We Christians are the unmistakable scent of Christ," is the way J. B. Phillips puts it. Through close association and growing intimacy with Christ, the very personalities of Paul and his friends had become impregnated with the fragrance the knowledge of Him imparted. In spreading His fragrance, our lives too can become aromatic.

> *A Persian fable says:*
> *One day*
> *A wanderer found a lump of clay*
> *So redolent of sweet perfume*
> *Its odor scented all the room.*
> *What art thou? was his quick demand*
> *Art thou some gem from Samarcand?*
> *Then whence this wondrous perfume, pray?*
>
> *Friend, if the secret I disclose,*
> *I have been living with the rose!*
> *Sweet parable. And will not those*
> *Who love to dwell with Sharon's rose*
> *Distil sweet odors all around*
> *Though low and mean themselves are found?*
> *Dear Lord, may we to Thee retreat,*
> *Then shed abroad Thy fragrance sweet.*
>
> Anonymous

THE COST OF THE FRAGRANCE

When we enjoy the sweetness of some delicate perfume, we seldom consider the cost at which it has been produced—thousands of flowers taken at the height of their beauty and crushed to capture their aroma for our delectation.

Some flowers and shrubs (lavender and rosemary) yield their fragrance only when they are crushed and bruised. Others (night-scented stock) release their perfume only under cover of the darkness of night. The aroma of incense is imprisoned until the flame kindles it.

Does this not find a parallel in life? Often the most fragrant Christians are those who have experienced the dark, crushing experiences of life. Believers who exude the fragrance of Christ are often those who have passed through the waters and fires of testing and have emerged triumphantly.

The fragrance of Christ flows preeminently from His Cross and suffering. The borrowed fragrance of Paul's life can be attributed to his experience of the fellowship of those sufferings. Nor will it be otherwise with us, for suffering rightly received will produce a maturity and sweetness of character that can be produced in no other way. Such lives are always unconsciously influential.

> *Not only in the words you say,*
> *Not only in your deeds expressed,*
> *But in the most unconscious way*
>   *Is Christ expressed.*
>
> *Is it a beatific smile,*
> *A holy light upon your brow?*
> *O no! I felt His presence*
>   *While you laughed just now.*
>
> *For me 'twas not the truth you taught,*
> *To you so clear, to me so dim,*
> *But when you came, you brought*
>   *A sense of Him.*
>
> *And from your eyes He beckons me,*
> *And from your heart His love is shed,*
> *'Til I lose sight of you and see*
>   *The Christ instead.*
>
>   Anonymous

On the day of his induction into the parish of Bremerton in 1630, George Herbert was a long time in returning to his vicarage after the ceremony. His friends found him alone in his new church. Lying prostrate in the chancel before the communion table, George Herbert appeared to be overwhelmed with the dignity and needs of his new charge. Unaware of the presence of his friends, he was silently worshiping. All they could hear him say was, "Jesus, my Master!"

Those who know George Herbert's poetry will recognize these lines from his *The Odour:*

How sweetly doth "My Master" sound, "My Master!"
As ambergris leaves a sweet scent unto the taster,
So do these words of sweet content,
An Oriental fragrancy—
*   "My Master!"*
With these all day I do perfume my mind.

A SOLEMN ASPECT

Our key passage speaks of two perfumes: one the smell of death, the other the fragrance of life; one a deadly fume, the other a delightful perfume. The solemn message Paul deduces is that the same glorious gospel message works both life and death—life to the one who receives it, death to the one who rejects it.

The picture of the triumphal march is still in Paul's mind. We are told that at the foot of the Capitoline Hill, the procession divided into two streams. One stream marched to the forbidding Tulanium where the doomed captives were put to death. The other stream marched on to life and liberty.

But the same perfume of fragrant incense pervaded both branches of the procession. To the one group it was the very smell of doom. To the other it was the fragrance of life abundant.

Since this is so, how solemn a thing it is to be a messenger of the gospel! The same gospel we preach is to some a delicious aroma; to others it is a noxious fume. The same sun melts the wax and hardens the clay. The preacher of the gospel should declare with Paul, "Knowing . . . the terror of the Lord, we persuade men" (2 Cor. 5:11 KJV).

NOTES

1. As quoted in George Armerding, *Fragrance Ascending* (Oakland: Western Book Co.), p. 3.
2. Ibid., p. 14.
3. Ibid., p. 52.

13

No Plow,
No Maturity

"Listen and hear my voice; pay attention and hear what I say. When a farmer plows for planting, does he plow continually? Does he keep on breaking up and harrowing the soil? When he has leveled the surface, does he not sow caraway and scatter cummin? Does he not plant wheat in its place, barley in its plot, and spelt in its field? His God instructs him and teaches him the right way. Caraway is not threshed with a sledge, nor is a cartwheel rolled over cummin; caraway is beaten out with a rod, and cummin with a stick. Grain must be ground to make bread; so one does not go on threshing it forever. Though he drives the wheels of his threshing cart over it, his horses do not grind it. All this also comes from the Lord Almighty, wonderful in counsel and magnificent in wisdom." —Isaiah 28:23–29

If there is to be a ripened harvest of spiritual maturity in our lives, we must expect the heavenly Plowman to use His plow and harrows in the soil of our hearts. No plow, no harvest.

The prophet Isaiah, under the inspiration of the Holy Spirit, uses this figure in a vivid and graphic manner. In this parable, the prophet uses the methods adopted by the farmer in producing a crop to illustrate the way in which God deals with His people. The primary application of the parable is doubtless to God's dealings with the nations, but the same principles apply to His activities in the church and in the lives of individuals.

Isaiah notes those attributes of God that so wonderfully characterize His discipline of His children. First, God instructs and teaches His child in the right way (Isa. 28:26). Second, God is wonderful in counsel. Third, God is magnificent in wisdom (Isa. 28:29). This means that everything He does is motivated by unconditional love and perfect wisdom. In achieving His purposes, He always acts with the keenest discrimination in the means He adopts.

The expertise and discretion of the farmer is exhibited in the processes he uses in gleaning a harvest—plowing and harrowing, sowing and reaping. His skill reflects the wisdom with which his God has endowed him. In lively language Isaiah argues that if in the superintending of his crops, the farmer displays such care and discernment, will the God who tutored him be less discriminating in His oversight of the much more delicate operation of gathering a spiritual harvest?

Three truths emerge from a study of the parable.

PLOWING

God, the heavenly Farmer, exercises the gentlest care when He permits the plow and harrows to invade our lives. He always keeps the ultimate purpose in mind—a golden harvest—and every part of the process is subservient to that end. He is, therefore, discerning in the duration of the discipline. "Does he keep on breaking up and harrowing the soil?" (Isa. 28:24b) asks the prophet. Of course not. Once the objective is achieved, the trial ends. His love will not permit one hour of suffering more than is essential to ensure the harvest.

Plow on, Lord, I want my life to be plowed all over, and that in every corner there may be golden grain or glorious flowers.

Pity me, Lord, when I exclaimed when I first felt the plowshare. Thou knowest my frame, Thou rememberest that I am dust.

But now I recollect, I put things together. I see Thy meaning. So, drive on, Thou Plowman of eternity!

Joseph Parker, *The Heavenly Plowman*

The farmer's experience helps him know what kind of treatment to give the various types of soil. Sandy loam requires light treatment, but the stiff clay necessitates the deep penetration of the plowshare into the subsoil. The harrows are used only until clods are broken and the soil is loose enough for the seeds to germinate. These are the factors that explain the unequal incidence of suffering and sorrow in the lives of God's children. We can entrust their timing to the loving discretion of our heavenly Father.

God's tilling of our lives always has our blessing and highest interests in view. "God disciplines us for our good, that we may share in his holiness" (Heb. 12:10). God's actions will bring only good when they are rightly received. The way in which we react will determine whether they sweeten or sour, whether they are bane or blessing. God never acts out of caprice.

Three possible reactions are open to us. We can *submit,* which is the fatalistic attitude of the Moslem. Since it is useless to resist, we can bow to God's actions. We can *acquiesce,* which is a passive acceptance, but often without joy. This is higher ground than mere submission, but it is not the highest. We can *embrace* God's actions with joy, even though we do not understand them. That is the highest ground. Paul demonstrated this attitude when he wrote: "I will boast all the more gladly about my weaknesses, so that Christ's power may rest upon me.

That is why, for Christ's sake, I delight in weaknesses, in insults, in hardships, in persecutions, in difficulties. For when I am weak, then I am strong" (2 Cor. 12:9b–10). It is this latter attitude that most glorifies God and brings peace and contentment to the heart.

Madame Jeanne de la Mothe Guyon was incarcerated in the infamous Bastille for ten years, from 1695–1705. What this must have meant to a delicately nurtured noblewoman may well be imagined. But what a harvest was reaped from her joyous acceptance of the trial! She describes her experience in these glowing words:

> *A little bird am I*
> *Shut out from fields of air,*
> *Yet in my cage I sit and sing*
> *To Him who placed me there;*
> *Well-pleased a prisoner to be,*
> *Because, my God, it pleaseth Thee.*

> *Naught else have I to do,*
> *I sing the whole day long,*
> *And He whom most I love to please*
> *Doth listen to my song.*
> *He caught and bound my wandering wing,*
> *And still He bends to hear me sing.*

> *My cage confines me round,*
> *Abroad I cannot fly,*
> *But though my wing is closely bound*
> *My heart's at liberty.*
> *My prison walls cannot control*
> *The flight, the freedom of the soul.*

> *O, it is good to soar*
> *These bolts and bars above,*
> *To Him whose purpose I adore,*

> *Whose providence I love,*
> *And in Thy mighty love to find*
> *The joy and freedom of the mind.*

SOWING

The farmer is careful in the selection and evaluation of the seeds, as well as in the choice of location for the sowing. "When he has leveled the surface, does he not sow caraway and scatter cummin? Does he not plant wheat in its place, barley in its plot, and spelt in its field?" (Isa. 28:25). He does not scatter his valuable seed indiscriminately or choose its location haphazardly. The most valuable crop is allotted the most fertile situation. Seeds of lesser value occupy odd corners.

Is God less discriminating in the experiences with which He entrusts us? He is selective about both soil and seed. He controls the timing. Sometimes He denies, sometimes He delays, but He is "wonderful in counsel and magnificent in wisdom" (Isa. 28:29). He intermingles joy with sorrow and adversity with prosperity, but He always has a harvest in view.

THRESHING

The threshing technique requires as great discretion as the sowing process. "Caraway is not threshed with a sledge, nor is a cartwheel rolled over cummin; caraway is beaten out with a rod, and cummin with a stick" (Isa. 28:27).

The farmer carefully notices the size and nature of the seed as well as its value, and he adapts his threshing method accordingly. Each seed requires special treatment. He does not use the heavy cartwheel when a light stick will suffice. The farmer's wisdom and experience hold him back from using excess force. His objective is not crushing the seed but freeing it from the useless chaff and straw. Will God be less discriminating? If the cartwheel is used, it is only because no other method will suffice. So God uses no more force than is absolutely essential to ensure a clean and valuable harvest. The spiritually mature Christian will accept and embrace the experience God allows and will not rebel against it. Paul attained a high level of maturity when he could say that he gloried in his tribulation (see Rom. 5:3).

From this parable there are three important lessons for us to learn about spiritual maturity.

First, the disciplines God uses in our lives are designed to produce a spiritual harvest, but the experience is not always pleasurable. "No discipline seems pleasant at the time, but painful. *Later on, however, it produces a harvest* of righteousness and peace for those who have been trained by it" (Heb. 12:11, italics mine).

Even God's Son could be brought to complete maturity in His humanity only in this way. "Although he was a son, he learned obedience from what he suffered and, once made perfect, he became the source of eternal salvation for all who obey him" (Heb. 5:8–9). Where discipline is not heeded, there is no harvest. God lavished His kindness on the Israelites, but they answered with rebellion, and there was no harvest of peace in their national life.

Second, our experience of God's discipline, when rightly reacted to, can bring life and blessing to others. "Grain must be ground to make bread, so one does not go on threshing it for ever" (Isa. 28:28). The grain is not bruised in the threshing process or its value would deteriorate, but it is ground to make bread. Grain in the husk is not acceptable for human consumption, it must be sifted and separated in the grinding process. Christ was bruised to become bread for us. "It is enough for . . . the servant [to be] like his master'' (Matt. 10:25). Bruising is part of the price of an enlarged ministry.

Bread Corn is bruised.
Shrink not, my soul
From the plucking and the binding,
From the breaking and the grinding.
The heart God breaks
He doth make whole.
The corn unshelled and thrown aside
Cannot for man's sore need provide.

Last, the disciplines God uses are always for our good and have eternal values in view. "God disciplines us for our good, that we may share in his holiness" (Heb. 12:10b). They are designed to prepare us for heaven. This life is heaven's kindergarten. Alexander Whyte wrote:

We cease to wonder so much at the care God takes of human character and the cost He lays out on it, when we think that it is the only work of His hands that shall last for all eternity.

If it is true that we are a garden or field cultivated by God, I am sure one of the best garden tools the Lord uses in our lives to produce fruit and stimulate growth is the digging trowel of suffering.

How hard it is to let him dig. Every time He uses suffering to cultivate and aerate the soil around us, we are sure our lives are being uprooted and bound for annihilation.

Yet quite the opposite is true. God uses His trowels and plows with the utmost discretion and wisdom, and all that digging produces healthy, growing people.[1]

NOTES

1. Joyce Landorf, *The High Cost of Growing* (New York: Nelson, 1978), p. 13.

14

Maturity
Demands Discipline

The fruit of the Spirit is self-control. —Galatians 5:23

"The world belongs to the disciplined." This statement may sound exaggerated, but it enshrines more than a grain of truth. Only the disciplined person will rise to the full potential of his or her powers. Only the person who is prepared to maintain a consistent self-discipline will experience a steadily increasing maturity.

A mature leader is able to give inspiring leadership to others because they sense that he or she is strongly disciplined, and they are, therefore, willing to accept the discipline expected of them.

The words *disciple* and *discipline* spring from the same root. A disciple is a disciplined person who has learned that lesson in the school of Christ. Thayer-Grimm define discipline as "a virtue which consists in mastering the appetites and passions, especially the sensual ones." It is this quality which so markedly differentiates humans from animals. Discipline is, however, the ugly duckling of modern psychology. The temper of the age is against it. Self-fulfillment and self-indulgence are the watchwords rather than self-discipline.

In the realm of sports, instead of participating, the vast majority merely watch and enjoy the fruit of the vicarious discipline of a handful of players. They shirk the rigors and sacrifice that excellence in sports demands. The digest and condensed book have displaced the work that demands mental discipline. So is it in the realm of the spirit.

The maturing Christian learns to submit to a discipline imposed from without, for if the believer has never mastered the lesson of being a good and loyal follower, he or she will not be fit to lead. But the Christian will also impose a more rigorous self-discipline from within. Those who neglect discipline in their lifestyle never attain full maturity of Christian character, and they will seldom qualify for influential leadership. Many who undertake training with a view to attaining important leadership positions fail because they have never learned to obey and follow a leader. Did not our Lord Himself have to "learn obedience by the things he suffered"?

When Benjamin Disraeli was prime minister of Britain, he made an important speech that had far-reaching effects in the political realm.

"May I ask how long it took to prepare that speech?" asked an admirer.

"All my life has been a preparation for the speech I made today," was the statesman's reply. A lifetime of study and mental discipline had equipped him to rise to the unexpected need of the moment. A life of discipline in early years, a life that is prepared to make renunciations and sacrifices to gain preparation for the life-task, will pave the way for high achievement.

The prayer of St. Augustine clearly indicates the importance he accorded to this quality:

> *O That I might have*
> *Towards my God, a heart of flame;*
> *Towards my fellow-men, a heart of love;*
> *Towards myself, a heart of steel.*

From the frequency with which the New Testament writers use Greek games as illustrations of the Christian life, it would seem clear that God desires us to do in the spiritual realm what the athlete does in the physical. Expressions like "he that strives for the mastery" (1 Cor. 9:25 KJV) and "every athlete exercises self-control in all things" (1 Cor. 9:25 RSV) indicate the seriousness with which the athlete pursues the objective. The pampered and flabby athlete wins no medals. The soft, self-indulgent Christian will not gain "the prize."

How do we "train" for the mature Christian life? Let us consider the "training" of the apostle Paul.

First, Paul imposed a rigorous discipline on his mind. He monitored his mental habits. "The weapons we fight with are not the weapons of the world. On the contrary, they have divine power to demolish strongholds. We demolish arguments and every pretension that sets itself up against the knowledge of God, *and we take captive every thought to make it obedient to Christ*" (2 Cor. 10:4–5, italics mine).

"Our voluntary thoughts not only reveal what we are—they predict what we will become," wrote A. W. Tozer. "The will can become the servant of the thoughts and to a large degree even our feelings follow our thinking. Thinking stirs feeling and feeling triggers action. This is the way we are made and we may as well accept it."

Sin has its genesis in the thought life, so Paul waged war with his thoughts. He made it his constant endeavor to make a prisoner of his fugitive thoughts and bring them under the control of Christ. It requires more than strong will power to bring and keep the mind under divine control, but provision has been made for this: "The fruit of the Spirit is self-control" (Gal. 5:23). Because Paul was full of the Spirit, this desirable fruit was produced in his life in abundance.

Paul's advice to the Christians in Philippi indicated the habit of his thought life: "Whatever is true, whatever is noble, whatever is right, whatever is pure, whatever is lovely, whatever is admirable—if anything is excellent or praiseworthy—*think about such things"* (Phil. 4:8, italics mine). And what a rich harvest he reaped in his intellectual life! Christ is worthy of our intellectual best.

Second, Paul exercised a stern discipline on his body. "I do not run like a man running aimlessly; I do not fight like a man beating the air. No, I beat my body and make it my slave so that after I have preached to others, I myself will not be disqualified for the prize" (1 Cor. 9:26–27).

In this statement Paul seems to be expressing a genuine fear. He was in no doubt about his salvation, but he had not yet completed his course. There was still time for his body to betray him. Despite his vast experience and great successes, he was still vulnerable in his body. So, in order that his ministry should not be short-circuited in his closing years, he continued to the end to maintain as strict a discipline in this area as the athlete does in his. He made his body his servant, not his master. This attitude is worthy of our emulation.

Shortly before Polycarp, bishop of Smyrna, was martyred, he prayed: "O God, make me a true athlete of Jesus Christ, to suffer and to conquer."

Paul exhorted Timothy, "Train yourself to be godly," or as J. B. Phillips puts it, "Take time and trouble to keep spiritually fit" (1 Tim. 4:7). "Everyone who competes . . . goes into strict training" (1 Cor. 9:25). For ten months athletes engaged in rigorous training in the Atlis gymnasium, and no one could compete until he had completed the full course. The athletes voluntarily abstained from certain pleasures and pastimes and had a spare and balanced diet. They got rid of superfluous fat.

Note that this discipline is not enforced but purely voluntary. The aspiring athlete willingly embraces it so that he may win the coveted prize. He loves his food but denies that which is too rich. He likes tobacco and beer, but to win the prize, he gives it up. He likes staying up late at night, but to attain maximum fitness, he goes to bed early.

He disciplines himself, not indulges himself. Thus will it be with the mature Christian athlete. Is there any of this intensity and dedication in our Christian life?

The consistent and strenuous self-discipline of the athlete for his fleeting prize—a crown of pine or laurel leaves—is a stinging rebuke to all half-hearted, reluctant service for God.

So discipline is training, whether imposed from without or from within, that produces obedience, self-control, and capacity for cooperation. Discipline extends to the mind and its thoughts, to the heart and its emotions, and to the body and its instincts. It "corrects, molds, and perfects mental faculties and character."

An increasingly disciplined lifestyle is evidence that the Holy Spirit is at work in our lives, for discipline is the fruit of the Spirit, not the work of the energetic self-life. It is not the control of self by self. Self is a hydra-headed monster that will take more than human power to subdue. Discipline is not stern self-suppression but the control of the redeemed life by the Holy Spirit: "For if you live according to the sinful nature, you will die; but if by the Spirit you put to death the misdeeds of the body, you will live" (Rom. 8:13). As we surrender our lives to the Spirit's control, He will keep our vagrant appetites in check.

God does not leave us dependent on our own slender resources, but He has made provision so that we can live lives that are wholesomely disciplined. "For God did not give us a spirit of timidity, but a spirit of power, of love, and self-discipline" (2 Tim. 1:7).

15

Maturity
of Conscience

*"So I strive always to keep my conscience clear before
God and man."* —Acts 24:16

In view of the vastly important role conscience fills,
especially in regard to our emotional well-being, it is
astounding that such slight attention is paid to the function
of this persistent monitor of the soul. This neglect is
difficult to understand in the light of the frequency of its
mention in Scripture. It is this faculty that differentiates
humans from animals.

Conscience is not easy to define. Is it a separate
faculty of our moral nature? Is it a divine and therefore
infallible endowment, or is it a fallible human mechanism?
A study of the relevant Scripture passages would appear to
indicate that conscience is a special activity of intellect and
emotions that enables its possessor not only to perceive
moral distinctions but also to discriminate between good
and evil.

One definition is that it is the testimony and judgment
of the soul that gives approval or disapproval to the
decisions and acts of the will. "When Gentiles, who do not
have the law, do by nature things required by the law, they
are a law for themselves, even though they do not have the
law, since they show that the requirements of the law are
written on their hearts, their consciences also bearing
witness, and their thoughts, now accusing, now even
defending them" (Rom. 2:14–15).

It is the activity of conscience that makes our sin culpable. The word signifies "knowledge held in conjunction with another," and of course the other is God. Conscience thus makes us co-witnesses with God against ourselves.

We must not, however, regard conscience as an executive faculty, for it is completely powerless to make us do right or keep us from doing wrong. Its sole responsibility and activity is to deliver its verdict according to its standards and produce the appropriate emotion. A thermometer would constitute a good parallel. It registers and indicates the temperature but has no power to create or modify it. If the verdict of conscience is ignored, there is nothing more it can do; but its sensitive mechanism is thereby damaged.

Conscience is not the privileged possession of only the advanced nations; it functions equally faithfully in the heart of ignorant pagans. When pagans violate the standards of their own culture, they are conscious of that inner voice expressing disapproval.

A missionary friend of mine once visited an African tribe that had had no previous contact with white people. Desiring to know the spiritual reactions of the chief, my friend asked the chief through an interpreter, what he thought sin was. Without hesitation the chief replied, "Sin is murder, theft, adultery, and witchcraft." His conscience bore faithful witness to the Law of God written on his heart.

Conscience is not infallible, for it can react only to the standards it knows. It is a safe guide only when it has been instructed by the Word of God. The consciences of the men who conducted the Inquisition commended them for perpetrating the horrors of that period. They reacted according to the accepted standard. The delicate mechanism of conscience was thrown off balance at the Fall and requires constant adjustment to God's standards. Conscience will react with varying degrees of accuracy according to the adjustment.

Paul speaks of a commending conscience and a condemning conscience.

A COMMENDING CONSCIENCE

Paul lists three progressive conditions of conscience. To enjoy the consistent commendation of our consciences is a priceless treasure—and conscience is just as faithful in commending the good as in condemning the evil.

A clear conscience

"They must keep hold of the deep truths of their faith with a clear conscience" (1 Tim. 3:9). "I thank God, whom I serve . . . with a clear conscience" (2 Tim. 1:3).

A clear conscience is one that is acutely sensitive to the approach of evil. Paul asserted that he had to strive to keep his conscience clear. It was not automatic. He maintained its purity by meticulous obedience to the dictates of Scripture and the promptings of the Holy Spirit.

When we are happy possessors of such a conscience, we experience no accusing voice to disturb the peace of God in our hearts, nor does it mar our relationships to others. A clear conscience leaves us with "a heart at leisure from itself, to soothe and sympathize." No price is too high to pay for such a boon.

A good conscience

"The goal of this command is love, which comes from a pure heart and a good conscience" (1 Tim. 1:5). "Holding on to faith and a good conscience" (1 Tim. 1:19). A good conscience commends the right and condemns the wrong. It is the possession of one who obeys the dictates of the clear conscience.

A *mature conscience*

"The gifts and sacrifices being offered were not able to clear the conscience of the worshiper. . . . How much more, then, will the blood of Christ, who through the eternal Spirit offered himself unblemished to God, cleanse our consciences from acts that lead to death, so that we may serve the living God!" (Heb. 9:9, 14).

Now with a good, clear, cleansed conscience the believer can give himself or herself without any sense of condemnation to the service of God.

A CONDEMNING CONSCIENCE

But Paul has another list of progressive conditions of conscience.

A *weak conscience*

A weak conscience tends to be morbid and overscrupulous and is easily upset by trifles. A weak conscience is chronically self-accusatory. Paul illustrates this from the problem of eating food that had been offered to idols. "Some people are still so accustomed to idols that when they eat such food they think of it as having been sacrificed to an idol, and since their conscience is weak, it is defiled" (1 Cor. 8:7).

Writing on this passage, Leon Morris commented: "Through being accustomed to idols before conversion, they still had the old associations though now Christians. Not being able to shake off the feeling that the idol was somehow real, they felt they were doing wrong when they ate what had been offered to it."[1]

The weak conscience reacts faithfully according to its light, but like a compass with a weak magnetic current, it gives an unsteady signal. This causes its possessor to be constantly tormented about whether he or she has done the wrong thing. One cause of this vacillation may be an inadequate knowledge of the Scriptures or a will that is not fully surrendered to God.

The corrective action would be to resolutely face the issues involved, make a decision according to one's best judgment, and then resolutely refuse to open the matter again.

A defiled conscience (see 1 Cor. 8:7)

If we willfully persist in engaging in some activity against which our conscience has protested, we thereby defile it and hinder its faithful functioning, just as dust in the mechanism of a watch will cause it to register the wrong time.

This is especially the case with moral purity. "To the pure, all things are pure, but to those who are corrupted and do not believe, nothing is pure. In fact, both their minds and consciences are corrupted" (Titus 1:15).

An evil or guilty conscience (see Heb. 10:22)

This condition results from habitual disregard of the warnings of conscience. It results in its possessor having his or her values so warped by indulgence in sin that the conscience is poisoned, and the person calls good evil and evil good. If the person is bent on doing evil, the voice of conscience will grow progressively more faint.

It is a well-known fact of criminology that a criminal guilty of shocking crimes against a person will often be tormented by his or her conscience because he or she betrayed to the police a companion in crime.

A seared conscience

"Such teachings come through hypocritical liars, whose consciences have been seared as with a hot iron" (1 Tim. 4:2). When conscience becomes so cauterized, it no longer protests at wrong, because no appeal will succeed. It is no longer sensitive to right and wrong.

> *Vice is a monster of such frightful mien*
> *That to be hated, needs but to be seen;*
> *But seen too oft, familiar with her face,*
> *We first endure, then pity, then embrace.*[2]

Paul warns of the peril of failing to heed and respond to the voice of conscience. "Fight the good fight," he says, "holding on to faith and a good conscience. Some have rejected these and so have shipwrecked their faith" (1 Tim. 1:19).

Conscience has no cure for its own ills, but we should be eternally grateful that adequate provision has been made for the maintenance of its purity and sensitivity.

A mature conscience accepts and rests upon the affirmations of the Word of God and refuses to resurrect what God has buried or to remember what God has forgotten. God has said, "I will forgive their wickedness and will remember their sins no more" (Heb. 8:12). Conscience rests on that assurance.

There is also a remedy for a defiled or guilty conscience, but there must be a sincere dealing with sin. The invitation is extended: "Let us draw near to God with a sincere heart in full assurance of faith, having our hearts sprinkled to cleanse us from a guilty conscience and having our bodies washed with pure water" (Heb. 10:22). John gives further assurance: "If we confess our sins, he is faithful and just and will forgive us our sins and purify us from all unrighteousness" (1 John 1:9).

> To continue condemning oneself for what God has forgiven is disloyalty to Christ. —Anonymous

How wonderful that the solvent of the blood of Christ applied to the guilty conscience removes every last stain and leaves the believer with a mature conscience, void of offense before God and others—conscience cleansed from all we have done and been. "Therefore, there is now no condemnation for those who are in Christ Jesus" (Rom. 8:1).

NOTES

1. Leon Morris, *The First Epistle to the Corinthians* (London: Tyndale House Publishers, 1958), p. 27.
2. Alexander Pope, *An Essay on Man,* Epistle ii, ll. 217–221.

16

The Place of Habit in Maturity

I put this in human terms because you are weak in your natural selves. Just as you used to offer the parts of your body in slavery to impurity and to ever-increasing wickedness, so now offer them in slavery to righteousness leading to holiness. —Romans 6:19

Paul here refers to the crucial part habit plays in the pursuit of Christian maturity. The former evil habits of the Roman Christians had to be reversed if they were to make progress in holiness. Just as in the past they had practiced evil habits, whether consciously or unconsciously, so now they must devote themselves to cultivating habits of holiness. The old verse is all too true to life:

> *Sow a thought, reap an act.*
> *Sow an act, reap a habit.*
> *Sow a habit, reap a character.*
> *Sow a character, reap a destiny.*

We are a bundle of habits. Character is made up of a cluster of habits, either good or bad. Habit-making and habit-breaking is one of our dominant activities. Every part of life is affected by the kind of habits we form. Each day we have to choose whether we will obey the dictates of the old or of the new nature, whether we will take the high road or the low road.

Habit has been defined as "training, especially of the

kind that produces self-control, orderliness, obedience, and capacity for cooperation." Another definition is: "the prevailing disposition or character of a person's feelings or a behavior pattern acquired by frequent repetition."

We can develop habits without any conscious act of the will. They are "thought, feeling, choice hardening into permanency."[1] An act begins by being occasional, but by frequent repetition it becomes habitual. A habitual criminal is one who, on being released from prison, repeats again and again the criminal actions.

DISROBING AND ROBING

Paul uses the figure of disrobing and robing to illustrate his point.

> You were taught, with regard to your former way of life, to *put off* your old self, which is being corrupted by its deceitful desires; to be made new in the attitude of your minds; and to *put on* the new self, created to be like God in true righteousness and holiness. —Ephesians 4:22–24, italics mine

Forming new and good habits is the best antidote to the old bad habits. The sinful disposition and habits formed over a lifetime are to be discarded like an old suit of clothes. This involves a decisive act of the renewed will. In addition, new and holy habits are to be adopted and donned like a new garment. This involves an equally decisive act of the will.

Have we not proved with monotonous regularity that the unaided human will is a broken reed to lean upon? We need only review our past New Year's resolutions to convince us of this fact. But ours is not an unregenerate will. It has been renewed by the Holy Spirit. In addition to this we have the promised aid of our God, for "it is God who works in you to will and to act according to his good purpose" (Phil. 2:13). God is here pledged to impart both the impulse and the power to achieve as we trust in Him for it.

I came recently on these lines that express the power of our will.

There is a field of earth, and standing in it a plough,
but unless a man will put his hand to the plough
and drive it straight forward, there will be no furrow.

There is a basket of seed laid beside the furrow,
but unless a man will take the basket and scatter
the seed in the furrow, there will be no harvest.

There is a field of ripe corn, and a sickle lies at hand,
but unless a man will seize that sickle and reap the
grain, there will be no wheat in the barn.

There is a wealth of grain, but unless a man
will handle the corn, the people may starve
within sight of a bursting granary.

God does His part—do yours!

Anonymous

The initiative lies with us. It is for us to choose, to exercise our will to break with old and wrong habits and cultivate new and holy ones. And when we sincerely set our weak wills in that direction, as we rely on Him, the Holy Spirit will impart the strength to break with the old and cherish the new.

OUR PART IN FORMING HABITS

Over the years many people have formed bad habits about time. They have no conscience about wasting their own time or that of others. Some people are habitually unpunctual. I worked with a fine young couple who were so consistent in their time habits that one could set one's watch by them. But that would mean always being five minutes late! They had formed the bad habit and had never attempted to break it. It would have been no more difficult to form the habit of being five minutes early, but motivation was lacking. Making such a radical change would involve a determined and sustained act of the will, which they were unprepared to do.

We should remember the encouraging fact that while God will not act instead of us—we must do the acting—He will cooperate with us in our purpose to conform to His will.

In the days of George Müller, that man of faith and prayer, a young man was facing the common problem of finding it difficult to rise sufficiently early in the morning to spend time with God. One day the young man had a bright idea. If he could prevail on someone who had power in prayer to pray that he would be able to get up earlier in the morning, his problem would be solved. He had heard of Mr. Müller's prayer and faith, so he attended one of his meetings. At the close the young man stated his problem and asked Mr. Müller if he would pray about this matter.

"Indeed I will not," responded Mr. Müller. The young man was surprised that so godly a man would be unwilling to enlist in such a worthy cause. After a few moments Mr. Müller said, "I'll tell you what I will do. If you will get one leg out of bed tomorrow morning, I will pray that God will enable you to get the other leg out."

That was sound theology. God will not assume a responsibility that is ours, but He will enable us to fulfill it as we move forward in obedience, even though we may be very conscious of our own weakness.

While temperament, heredity, and environment all have a significant influence on our habits, the regenerated will, energized by the Holy Spirit is the determining factor. We are what we choose to be.

OUR PART IN BREAKING HABITS

Forming a new habit often involves breaking an old one, and this is no light task. The established pattern of the years will not be easily changed. We will need the powerful aid of the Holy Spirit if we are to break the sinful habits of the past.

Like the believers at Philippi, we can cultivate new habits of thought that will oust the former habits that led to sin. Every temptation comes to us by way of our thoughts. These, if evil, must therefore be replaced by wholesome thoughts in keeping with the mind of Christ. Hence Paul's exhortation:

> Finally, brothers, whatever is true, whatever is noble, whatever is right, whatever is pure, whatever is lovely, whatever is admirable—if anything is excellent or praiseworthy—*think about such things.* —Phillippians 4:8, italics mine

Once again the initiative is ours. We choose what thoughts fill our minds. Because this is commanded by God, it must be possible for us to conform. We can cultivate new habits of speech, for example. If we have been in the habit of exaggerating, embroidering the truth, telling untruths, or making insincere or inaccurate statements, we must resolutely form the habit of abjuring all these things and become scrupulously truthful and strictly honest in speech. We are exhorted to "put off all falsehood" and to "put on the girdle of truth."

Erwin Lutzer tells the story of a man who had been released from prison but was having difficulty adjusting to his freedom. He tried this experiment.

He took a glass bottle with a distinctive shape and crammed it full of wires, some small, some large. After some time had passed, he took a hammer and smashed the bottle. The result? Most of the wires retained the shape of the bottle and had to be straightened out one by one.

The man established his point. It is possible to be free and still retain the traits of bondage. Even though a man is liberated, he must adjust to his freedom and carefully dismantle the habits of the past.[2]

Each sin we commit only serves to strengthen the habits of sin we have acquired. Every time an alcoholic drinks alcohol, the more he or she is enslaved by it. On the other hand, every time the alcoholic says "No" to the temptation to sin, the more the desire to refuse is reinforced.

"It is by willing persistence and prayerful obedience to the requirements of Scripture," writes Jay Adams, "that godly patterns are developed and become part of us."

It was because Joseph had maintained a strong sense of personal purity that he came out unscathed from the seductions of Potiphar's wife. His fixed attitude was, "How can I sin against God in this way?" Good habits formed over a period of time will stand us in good stead in the hours of crisis.

Writing about this, Alexander Maclaren said, "The most advanced Christian life needs a perpetual renewal and repetition of past acts of faith. It cannot live on the past any more than the body can subsist on last year's food. We must gather fresh manna daily.

"The life is continued by the same means as that by which it began. There is no new duty or method for the most advanced Christian, he has to do just what he has been doing for half a century."

So then there is an element in habit breaking and habit making that is peculiarly our own. God will not do for us what He has planned and stated we must do for ourselves. It is a cooperative operation between God and us, a partnership, just as in nature we cooperate with God—not the one without the other.

NOTES

1. Arthur T. Pierson, *Godly Self-control* (Three Hills: Alberta, Canada, Prairie Bible Institute, 1980), p. 93.
2. Erwin Lutzer, "Those Sins That Won't Budge," *Moody Monthly* (March, 1978), p. 48.

17

Mature
Christian Conduct

Therefore, I urge you, brothers, in view of God's mercy, to offer your bodies as living sacrifices, holy and pleasing to God—which is your spiritual worship. Do not conform any longer to the pattern of this world, but be transformed by the renewing of your mind. Then you will be able to test and approve what God's will is—his good, pleasing, and perfect will. —Romans 12:1–2

The maturity of a Christian will be evidenced not only in character but also in conduct. The mature believer will act in a way that will commend Christ in everything, thus making his or her witness to Christ credible.

Romans 12 could be termed a compendium of Pauline ethics, covering most areas of life and human relationships. In characteristic fashion Paul follows his doctrinal dissertation in Romans 1–11 with pungent and practical application in Romans 12–16. Conduct must be brought into line with creed. Romans 12 is one of Paul's most perceptive treatments of Christian conduct.

THE IMPELLING MOTIVE

Romans 12 opens with an urgent appeal to the Roman Christians to offer their bodies to God as a living sacrifice, a worthy response to the mercy He had extended to them.

The verb "offer" or "present," as the Greek aorist tense suggests, indicates an initial crisis, a decisive act of presentation. It is a technical, priestly word that was used of offering a sacrifice at the temple—a single, definite act of dedication that should need no repetition.

Paul sees the motive for such a far-reaching and revolutionary action, in "the mercy of God," which he had been expounding in the previous eleven chapters. He never lost his sense of wonder at the kindness and love of God that had been extended unconditionally to him, the worst of sinners. "For I . . . do not even desire to be called an apostle, because I persecuted the church of God" (1 Cor. 15:9), he protested. Yet Paul had obtained mercy, and he wanted to live out his gratitude. The only worthy response to such mercy was to place all his ransomed powers at the disposal of his Master.

The aorist tense of verse 1 is followed by thirty-six present-tense verbs—a series of repeated acts that should follow the initial act of dedication. The act of presentation is an intensely practical thing with far-reaching implications. It centers on bodies that are the instruments of our minds and spirits. Formerly they were instruments of sin, but now they are laid on the altar and are to be left there. "Just as you used to offer the parts of your body in slavery to impurity and to ever-increasing wickedness, so now offer them in slavery to righteousness leading to holiness" (Rom. 6:19).

Unlike the Greek philosophers who despised the body, Christians honor it because it is the temple of the Holy Spirit. The fact that the Son of God condescended to take human form and live in a human body refutes the Greek attitude.

NON-CONFORMITY

The mature believer, delivered from the old lifestyle, no longer conforms to the pattern of this evil world. "Do not let the world squeeze you into its mold," is J. B. Phillips' translation of verse 2. We are not to adopt the protective coloration of the chameleon as we move in different environments. To speak of a "worldly Christian" is as much an anomaly as to speak of a "truthful liar" or an "honest thief." The words are antithetical and logically are mutually exclusive.

If we are mature Christians we will not cover ourselves over with the veneer of this age—we will be nonconformists where worldly standards and practices are concerned. We will not allow the world to write our agenda or decide what we should do or be.

Instead, we will be "transformed," changed from within. "Cease adapting yourself to this present age," Paul exhorts, "but continue your transformation by renewal of your mind." This inward renewal will involve a change in thinking and viewing things. The renewal will not be a sudden metamorphosis but a process initiated and stimulated by a dedicated will and empowered by the Holy Spirit.

This almost sounds as if the apostle is advocating a process of sanctification by self-effort, but in fact he is only recognizing that the mind has been affected by the Fall and must be renewed by the Holy Spirit. In this, the full cooperation of the believer is required. We must *keep on* repudiating the standards of the world and coming back to our original commitment. This is a rational rather than an emotional exercise—"Your reasonable service."

With our minds thus renewed, we will then be able to "test and approve God's will" for us and will find it to be good, pleasing, and perfect. It could not be otherwise, since it is the expression of perfect love and infinite knowledge.

THE GOLDEN MEAN

The key to Romans 12 is found in verse 3 in which there is in the Greek a play on words:

> For by the grace given in me I say to every one of you: Do not think of yourself more highly than you ought, but rather think of yourself with sober judgment, in accordance with the measure of faith God has given you.

E. M. Blaiklock suggests that the English verbs "to think," "to overthink," "to think sanely," capture the meaning of the passage. The thought is obviously that of modest self-appraisal. Instead of being conceited, the believer will think soundly and cultivate Christian sanity.

The Greek word *sophrosune,* which occurs in this passage, expresses that ideal balance of mind that never flies to extremes. The word has the meaning of moderation and self-control. To the Greeks this was a fundamental virtue, the golden mean between two extremes. As such, it is delicately poised and can slip either way very easily. For example, the virtue of courage can slip in one direction and degenerate into rashness, or it can slip in the other direction and become cowardice. The virtue of purity can become either prudery on the one hand or impurity on the other.

This ideal balance of mind is to be worked out in all of life's relations. This balance will enable us to rightly esteem God, ourselves, and our abilities and vocation "with sober judgment according to the faith God has given."

A FUNCTIONING BODY

With his accustomed insight, Paul uses the figure of the body to link doctrine with ethics. He turns his readers' attention away from purely individualistic thinking and reminds them that they are part of a Christian society. In the functioning of a human body, Paul finds an ideal picture of the unity, diversity, and mutuality that are to characterize relationships within the church.

> Just as each of us has one body with many members, and these members do not all have the same function, so in Christ we who are many form one body, and each member belongs to all the others. —Romans 2:4–5

This is a charming picture of mutuality and interdependence. The balance of mind will lead us to bear and forbear with the actions of others and to have a modest estimate of our own gifts. We will accept ourselves as we are, and will do all in our power to be what God wants us to be. As we do this in dependence on the Spirit, we will be progressively changed into Christ's likeness (see 2 Cor. 3:18). We will avoid both extremes of self-exaltation and self-depreciation.

SPIRITUAL GIFTS

> We have different gifts, according to the grace given us. If a man's gift is prophesying, let him use it in proportion to his faith. If it is serving, let him serve; if it is teaching, let him teach; if it is encouragement, let him encourage; if it is contributing to the needs of others, let him give generously; if it is leadership, let him govern diligently; if it is showing mercy, let him do it cheerfully. —Romans 12:6–8

Spiritual gifts come from the triune God and are to be exercised in and for the benefit of the church. "Having these gifts, let us use them." We must not allow these divinely bestowed gifts to atrophy through disuse. This was doubtless the thought behind Paul's double exhortation to Timothy: "Do not neglect your gift"; "Stir up your gift" (1 Tim. 4:14; 2 Tim. 1:6).

Prophecy stands at the head of the list, as it does in the other categories of spiritual gifts in the Epistles. The primary meaning of prophecy is the proclamation of the will of God in a manner that will at once convict and build up the hearers. It may also be the foretelling of future events under the inspiration of the Spirit.

As used in the New Testament, prophecy is the inspired exposition of the truth—speaking under the influence of the Holy Spirit rather than as the outcome of study and experience. It is a gift that can be controlled (see 1 Cor. 14:32).

Service is a broad term that includes administration and other practical services. For these there is abundant scope in church and community. The word was used of the household of Stephanas who "devoted themselves to the service of the saints" (1 Cor. 16:15)—apparently ministering to their physical needs. It is significant that this gift comes second on this list of spiritual gifts. Fortunately for us, the body is not all tongue!

Teaching differs from prophecy in that teaching is systematic instruction and exhortation that springs from the study of the Word of God. The message needs explanation as well as proclamation, and this is the teacher's special role. The teacher supplies the believers with material to make their private study more meaningful.

Encouraging, while allied to teaching and often accompanying it, has another dimension. Teaching instructs the mind, but it can be cold and factual and leave the emotions and will unmoved. Happy the teacher who combines the gifts of exhortation and encouragement. Those gifts, when linked with love and attractive example, can inflame the heart with love to God and others. It was this gift that made Barnabas the magnificent leader he became.

When he was an old man, Dr. F. B. Meyer affirmed that if he had his ministry to do over again, he would devote much more time to the ministry of comfort and encouragement.

There is a type of exhortation, however, that tends to be denunciatory and negative. This exhortation is anything but encouraging and leaves the hearers depressed rather than uplifted. There must be a faithful dealing with sin, but it is the tone in which it is done that is important. The purpose of encouragement is to spur people on to greater endeavor, achievement, and holiness.

Liberality, contributing generously to the needs of others, can have a spiritual dimension that adds greatly to the blessing it brings. It has been said that a sin lurks behind every virtue, and in this matter the danger would be an unworthy motivation. It is not so much what we give, as why.

We are not to give in the hope of gain or advantage to ourselves, but we are to give out of sheer love of God and love for those around us. As R. G. Le Tourneau once said, "If you give to God because it pays to be generous, it will not pay." Our benevolence is to be spontaneous, generous, and private.

Leadership. "If you are a leader, exert yourself to lead," is the New English Bible rendering of this clause in Romans 12:8. Lead with zeal and enthusiasm. One danger built into leadership would appear to be sloth and lethargy. Leadership demands exertion beyond the ordinary. True leaders will ask of others no sacrifice they are not prepared to make themselves. They will regard their leadership as an avenue of service rather than a position that confers prestige.

Showing mercy is not usually regarded as a spiritual gift, and yet it is so classified here. Often it is associated with the pastoral gift, and it includes ministry to the sick and needy in the community. The messengers of mercy will bring brightness and cheer to those who are burdened and suffering. In this the mercy-givers can expect the special aid of the Holy Spirit who imparted the gift.

In our Lord's life, we are told that "God anointed Jesus of Nazareth with the Holy Spirit and power" (Acts 10:38a). For what purpose? "He went around doing good, and healing all who were under the power of the devil" (Acts 10:38b). For this ministry He received this special equipment. The ministers of mercy can claim a similar anointing.

Genuine love. "Love must be sincere" (Rom. 12:9). "Love" is a word that has been sadly debased in contemporary society. In Scripture it stands very high in God's scale of virtues. This is necessarily so since "love is of God," and "God is love."

Christian love is to be genuine and utterly sincere—free from shame and hypocrisy. The family of God must exhibit mutual affection (Rom. 12:10). But Christian love is still a love that will neither condone evil nor overlook the good. Hating evil without loving the good engenders pride, while the reverse makes one a soft sentimentalist. Here again there must be that Christian balance of mind that flies to neither extreme. When we love in this way, there will be no room for a sense of superiority or pride. We will gladly honor others above ourselves.

18

The Spirit's Help
Toward Maturity

Now the Lord is the Spirit, and where the Spirit of the Lord is, there is freedom. And we, who with unveiled faces all reflect the Lord's glory, are being transformed into his likeness with ever-increasing glory, which comes from the Lord, who is the Spirit. —2 Corinthians 3:17–18

Let us be borne on to maturity. —Hebrews 6:1 (WESTCOTT)

As in every other aspect of the Christian life, the Holy Spirit plays a vital part in bringing the believer to maturity. Many people are much less clear in their conception of the person and work of the Holy Spirit than they are of the other two members of the Trinity. The use of the Old English term "Holy Ghost" in the King James Version of the Bible has tended to foster the element of mystery that tends to surround the Holy Spirit. But Scripture is very clear and explicit concerning His divine personality and His ministry in the life of the Christian.

The Holy Spirit is a divine person who is *exactly like Jesus.* When our Lord told His disciples that He would shortly leave them, they were devastated. For three years their lives had revolved around Him. How could they live without Him? To His sorrowing followers Jesus gave a reassuring promise:

> If you love me, you will obey what I command. And
> I will ask the Father, and he will give you another
> Counselor [Paraclete] to be with you forever—the
> Spirit of truth. . . . I will not leave you as orphans; I
> will come to you. —John 14:15–18

The Greek word for "another" here means "another
of exactly the same kind," and the word Paraclete is used
both of Jesus and of the Holy Spirit (see 1 John 2:1). So
Jesus was promising that after He ascended into heaven,
the One He would send to represent Him would be a
Paraclete exactly like Himself—His other self. This means
that the Holy Spirit can be known (see John 14:17) and
loved and obeyed in the same way as Jesus Himself. Does
this not bring Him very near to us?

The Holy Spirit is involved in every phase of our
spiritual life and experience. It was He who inspired the
Scriptures and now illumines them to our minds. He
convicts of sin, righteousness, and judgment. He regener-
ates and imparts new life. He sanctifies, unites to Christ,
and makes us progressively holy as we yield to His
promptings. He is the spirit of prayer and helps us in our
weakness in this area. He produces fruit in character and
empowers for effective witness. It is He who changes us
into the likeness of Christ—and this is spiritual maturity.

PENTECOST'S TRANSFORMING EXPERIENCE

After the descent of the Holy Spirit on the Day of
Pentecost, there was a noticeable acceleration in the
progress of the disciples' maturity. Before that epochal
event, the marks of spiritual immaturity were all too
evident in their lives and service. They were just average,
ordinary men of their day. All were slow learners (see
Luke 24:45). They were self-seeking (see Mark 10:37, 41).

They were paralyzed with fear of the Jews (see John 20:19). In Jesus' hour of deepest need at the Cross, they all "deserted him and fled" (Mark 14:50). They were ordinary, weak, failing men and women, very much like us.

But when at Pentecost "they were all filled with the Holy Spirit" and abandoned themselves to His control, a startling transformation took place. The timid became brave and the weak powerful. Doubters became believers and the selfish self-forgetful. Slow learners became avid scholars. Individualists became willing to submerge themselves in team ministry.

They all became vividly conscious of Christ's presence with them. Joy and thanksgiving were the keynotes of their corporate life (see Acts 2:46–47). In their previous ministry they had caused little stir, but now they gained the reputation of being "the men who have turned the world upside down."

While Pentecost, like Calvary, was an historical and never-to-be-repeated event, it can and should be perpetuated. All the external accompaniments may not be duplicated, but the inner power and thrust can be reproduced whenever we are prepared to conform to the laws of spiritual power.

THE SPIRIT HELPS TOWARD MATURITY

The Holy Spirit aids us in our progress toward maturity in several ways. Hebrews 6:1, "Let us go on to maturity," can with equal propriety be translated, "let us be borne on to maturity." The implication is that we are not left to do it by ourselves. We read in 2 Corinthians 3:18 that this transformation comes from the Lord, who is the Spirit. As the Paraclete, He is alongside us to help us, as that word implies. How does He help us?

The Holy Spirit reveals Christ to us

"When the Counselor comes, . . . he will testify about me." —John 15:26

"He [Holy Spirit] will bring glory to me by taking from what is mine and making it known to you." — John 16:14

These are direct promises of both revelation and illumination. The ministry of the Holy Spirit is essentially Christo-centric. His great objective is to magnify Christ and to secure in the lives of His followers practical recognition of His Lordship. Insofar as this is also our objective, we can confidently count on His fullest cooperation. It is no concern of His to make *us* great, but to reveal Christ's greatness.

Just as a telescope does not exist to reveal itself but only the object on which it is trained, so the Holy Spirit stands in the background and draws attention to Christ. A study of the Scriptures—both Old and New Testaments— reveals that every road leads to Christ. As we honor Him, the Holy Spirit will honor our witness to Christ and set His seal on it.

The Holy Spirit guides us into the will of God

If you are led by the Spirit . . . —Galatians 5:18

Since we live by the Spirit, let us keep in step with the Spirit. —Galatians 5:25

The Holy Spirit knows what the will of God is in every situation, for He "intercedes for the saints in accordance with God's will" (Rom. 8:26, 27).

The Holy Spirit guides primarily through the Scriptures that He has caused to be written and preserved for us. In them there is instruction about every area of life— moral and ethical principles, guidance in marital and family relationships, teaching about social conduct, and above all, infallible teaching in all areas of spiritual life.

The Holy Spirit further leads us into the will of God by influencing our mental processes as we submit our minds to His control. John Wesley testified that God generally guided him by presenting reasons to his mind for acting in a certain way. When once we have arrived at the best decision we can make in the light of all the facts and circumstances, we should strenuously resist the temptation to dig up in unbelief what we have sown in faith.

Where there is no explicit instruction in Scripture about the matter under consideration, the Holy Spirit will guide those who are genuinely willing to do His will (see John 7:17) by granting an inner conviction of the right way to act.

The Holy Spirit enables us to keep Christ on the throne of our lives

> *No one who is speaking by the Spirit of God says, "Jesus be cursed," and no one can say, "Jesus is Lord," except by the Holy Spirit.* —1 Corinthians 12:3

If the latter statement is interpreted with wooden literalism, then it is not true. An unconverted person can repeat those words. The tense of the verb, however, conveys the following sense: "No one can *keep on saying* 'Jesus is Lord' of my life except by the Holy Spirit's enabling." That carries with it the assurance that the Spirit's enabling is available for this purpose.

Even after we have genuinely enthroned Christ in our hearts (see 1 Pet. 3:15), it is all too easy to withdraw our allegiance if the inducement is sufficiently strong. But with the Holy Spirit in control of our wills, we have power not only to withstand the seductions of world, flesh, and devil, but also to keep Christ on the throne.

The Holy Spirit changes us into Christ's likeness

We, who with unveiled faces all reflect the Lord's glory, are being transformed into the same likeness with ever-increasing glory, which comes from the Lord who is the Spirit. —2 Corinthians 3:18

Here is the plain assertion that while we are spending time contemplating the glories and virtues of Christ, the Holy Spirit is progressively changing us into His likeness. We become like those we admire. As we look and long and pray to be more like Christ, without any conscious volition on our part, the Holy Spirit works into the fabric of our lives the very virtues and graces of the One we most admire and love—"We are being changed into the same likeness."

The process of digestion affords an interesting parallel. We ingest our food—and forget about it. Then, altogether apart from any conscious volition on our part, the digestive organs take over and change the food into blood and bone and tissue. In just the same way, while we spend time contemplating Christ in all His glory and graces, the Holy Spirit takes the very qualities we see and admire in Him and works them into the warp and woof of our spiritual lives. This "likeness" has two parts.

First, *the objective vision* of the glory of the Lord as it is revealed in all the Scriptures—His perfect manhood, flawless character, unique person, unconditional and undemanding love, and above all His mediatorial work (in short, the moral excellence ·of His character and conduct)—is progressively reproduced in us.

> *Show me Thy face! One transient gleam*
> *Of loveliness divine,*
> *And I shall never think or dream*
> *Of other love save Thine;*
> *All lesser light will darken quite,*
> *All lower glories wane,*

The beautiful of earth will scarce
Seem beautiful again.

Show me Thy face! My faith and love
Shall henceforth fixed be,
And nothing more have power to move
My soul's serenity.
My life shall seem a trance, a dream,
And all I feel and see
Illusive, visionary,
Thou art the one Reality.

Anonymous

The objective vision then issues in *a subjective transformation*—"We are being changed into the same likeness." God is not satisfied with us as we are. Nor should we be satisfied with ourselves, for we have been predestined "to be conformed to the likeness of His Son" (Rom. 8:29), and we have a long way to go.

This will be achieved not by external imitation but by internal transformation. With what end in view? The word "contemplate" in our text can also be rendered "reflect." We behold, contemplate His glory and then reflect it to others. "Those who look to him are radiant," said the psalmist (Psa. 34:5).

At the turn of the century, Rev. George C. Grubb, a saintly Anglican minister, was God's instrument in the conversion of hundreds of people in Australia and New Zealand. When traveling by ship from India to Australia, he followed the custom of taking an after-breakfast walk around the deck. He possessed great charm, and people responded as he smiled at them.

A mother with a little girl was approaching, and he beamed at them. After they had passed, the little girl said to her mother, "Mummie, was that Jesus?"

Here was someone who matched her childish conception of what Jesus would be like. We might well covet some of that charm or that of the unconscious radiance of Moses.

> When Moses came down from Mount Sinai with the two tablets of the Testimony in his hands, he was not aware that his face was radiant because he had spoken with the Lord. —Exodus 34:29

The Holy Spirit enables us to live and walk in the Spirit

> *So I say, live by the Spirit, and you will not gratify the desires of the sinful nature.* —Galatians 5:16

> *Since we live by the Spirit, let us keep in step with the Spirit.* —Galatians 5:25

> *For the sinful nature desires what is contrary to the Spirit, and the Spirit what is contrary to the sinful nature.* —Galatians 5:17

It is one thing to step out into the Christian life but quite another to maintain a consistent and intimate walk with God. The step must lengthen out into a walk, and this will demand both purpose and discipline.

In the above passages, living and walking in the Spirit are put in apposition to walking after the desires of our sinful natures. Two different Greek words are used in verses 16 and 25 for "walk," as it is translated in the King James Version.

The first is the ordinary word for walking about, and it refers to our conduct in ordinary life, our daily activities. We are to live in awareness that our bodies are temples of the Holy Spirit. The passage might be rendered, "habitually order your lifestyle through the Spirit's guidance, and then you will not be deflected by the desires of your sinful nature."

The second word means, "a measured walk," as in marching in step or in file, walk as an army walks. It carries the idea of joint effort or concerted action, and in this it is the Holy Spirit who is to lead. "If you are led by the Spirit, you are not under law" (Gal. 5:18). The tense of the verb in verse 25 gives the meaning: "Let us go on walking in the Spirit" as a settled habit, obeying His leading and depending on His power.

When verses 16 and 25 are taken together, they imply that we are to recognize the Spirit as the Guide in our personal lives in all our decisions and actions. When we engage in joint or concerted action, it is still the Spirit who is to guide and discipline our controlled effort.

When we make mistakes in our personal lives or when our relationships with others are fractured, the implication is that we have either not sought the guidance of the Spirit, or we have not been obedient to His promptings.

19

The New Covenant Enables Maturity

Now if the ministry that brought death . . . came with glory . . . will not the ministry of the Spirit be even more glorious? —2 Corinthians 3:7–8

But God found fault with the people and said: "The time is coming, declares the Lord, when I will make a new covenant with the house of Israel and with the house of Judah. . . . This is the covenant I will make with the house of Israel after that time, declares the Lord. I will put my laws in their minds and write them on their hearts. I will be their God, and they will be my people. No longer will a man teach his neighbor, or a man his brother, saying 'Know the Lord,' because they will all know me, from the least of them to the greatest. For I will forgive their wickedness and will remember their sins no more." —Hebrews 8:8, 10–12

The mature Christian has exchanged the futility and frustration of living under the old covenant of Law for the freedom and joy of the new covenant of grace. The dead hand of a law that brought only death and condemnation has relaxed its grip and given way to a higher law that brings life and liberation.

A covenant is a mutual agreement of binding force that puts an end to uncertainty. But in reality, the covenants that men and women enter into are evidence of mistrust rather than of trust. It is a mutual lack of confidence in each other that demands a formal undertaking. How gracious of our God to meet us on this low level!

THE OLD COVENANT

The covenant that God entered into with Abraham (and later confirmed to Moses) was *imperfect,* not because of any inherent defect, but because it was conditional on obedience, an obedience men and women constantly failed to render. The covenant was *impotent* because it imparted no dynamic for obedience. As Paul asserted, "For what the law was powerless to do in that it was weakened by the sinful nature, God did by sending his own Son . . ." (Rom. 8:3). Further, the covenant was *impossible* to keep, because "those controlled by the sinful nature cannot please God" (Rom. 8:8).

Then why did God make such a covenant? The old covenant of law was *educational* in purpose. It aimed to awaken in God's people a sense of their own innate inability to live a holy life and of their own inherent sinfulness—their total inability to cope, unaided, with the sin of their own nature. The old covenant was *external,* a series of stern legal prohibitions and negations with which the people discovered they could not comply. Inevitably it led them to the experience that Paul describes in such poignant terms:

> So I find this law at work: When I want to do good, evil is right there with me. For in my inner being I delight in God's law; but I see another law at work in the members of my body, waging war against the law of my mind and making me a prisoner of the law of sin at work within my members. What a wretched man I am! Who will rescue me from this body of death?
> —Romans 7:21–24

THE NEW COVENANT

Both Jeremiah and Ezekiel, each of whom had experienced the bondage and hopelessness of the old covenant, foresaw by divine illumination that a new day would dawn that would usher in a new and better covenant; one that would remedy the defects of the old. The glory of the new covenant consisted in the fact that it would not only demand but also empower. In short, it would be a covenant that would ensure against failure on humanity's side.

In face of the divine command, "Be holy, for I am holy," the believer struggling against the tyranny of sin grows discouraged by the inability to overcome. "It is not God's ability to deliver me from my sin that I doubt," the believer mourns; "It is my own deplorable weakness that I fear." It was to meet this very objection and to provide both motivation and dynamic for obedience that God instituted the new covenant. Its provisions were exactly tailored to the need of men and women who had failed.

In contra-distinction to the old covenant, which was *external,* imposed from without, the new covenant is *internal,* "written not with ink but with the Spirit of the living God, not on tablets of stone but on tablets of human hearts" (2 Cor. 3:3). Further, it contains the reassuring promise that the very disposition to do the will of God will be imparted.

In the old covenant the key expressions are: "Thou shalt, Thou shalt not." The key expression of the new is God's gracious, "I will." What the old demands, the new provides and enables.

With our background of knowledge of the doctrine of grace, it is difficult for us to envisage how startling and unbelievable these revolutionary provisions must have seemed to the Jews who for centuries had been crushed under the intolerable burden of the Law with the accompanying rabbinical accretions. To them it came as a totally new and incredible concept, the total reversal of all they had believed and practiced.

Ezekiel adds some other equally startling promises:

> "I will sprinkle clean water on you, and you will be clean; I will cleanse you from all your impurities and from all your idols. I will give you a new heart and put a new spirit in you; I will remove from you your heart of stone and give you a heart of flesh. And I will put my Spirit in you and move you to follow my decrees and be careful to keep my laws." —Ezekiel 36:25–27

It is a mark of maturity when Christians appropriate and rejoice in the deliverance from the bondage of their self-effort, which had been their disappointing experience under the old covenant, and begin to revel in the liberty of the new. No longer are they left to their own puny and unaided strivings to attain an elusive holiness. How they rely on the increasing and unceasing activity of the Holy Spirit in their lives. This is life indeed.

BLESSINGS OF THE NEW COVENANT

The new covenant is described as "a better covenant." In what senses is it better than the old? Here are some of the benefits it bestows:

Spiritual apprehension

> *"I will put my laws in their minds."* —Hebrews 8:10

God knows where to begin. The unfaithful priesthood of those days had failed dismally as interpreters of the Law. They could not convey to the people its inner meaning. But with the coming of the new covenant this defect was remedied. The Holy Spirit would open their eyes to perceive the nuances, the inner meaning of the Law, even as Christ did in His Sermon on the Mount.

Spiritual aspiration

> *"I will write them [my laws] on their hearts."*
> —Hebrews 8:10

Ezekiel had described their hearts as "hearts of stone," cold and unresponsive, rebellious and obdurate. But now comes the promise, "I will give you *a new heart* ... I will remove from you your heart of stone and give you a heart of flesh," soft and impressionable (Ezek. 36:26, italics mine). God will give us a heart in which aspiration is matched by desire.

God has written His law in the hearts of migratory birds. So indelibly is it engraved there that we can set our calendars by the date of their migration and return. He has so indelibly written His law in the heart of the pine cone that it can reproduce only pine trees. Should it be thought an incredible thing that God can write His law in our hearts? What He has done in nature, can He not do in grace?

Spiritual affinity

> *"You will be my people, and I will be your God."*
> —Ezek. 36:28.

> *"I will put my Spirit in you."* —Ezekiel 36:27.

What a sublime privilege! To be indwelt by the triune God! Nothing is of greater importance to growth in the Christian life than our relationship to God. This is the transcendent promise of the new covenant. It has been well said that God has not given His children the universe—that would be too small. He has given us Himself.

Spiritual attainment

> *"They will all know me, from the least of them to the greatest."* —Hebrews 8:11

The knowledge of God here promised is not so much the product of external teaching and study as of inward illumination. Was this not one of the accompaniments of the gift of the Holy Spirit on the Day of Pentecost?

In Peter's flaming sermon, he gave evidence that old Scripture that he had memorized now glowed with new meaning. Under the illumination of the Spirit, he grasped the meaning of prophecies that heretofore had been a closed book to him (see Acts 2:14–16).

We, too, have "an anointing from the Holy One, and all of you know the truth," wrote John (1 John 2:20). Under His teaching, God can become the One we know best.

Spiritual absolution

> *"I will forgive their wickedness and will remember their sins no more. . . ."* —Hebrews 8:12

> *"I will sprinkle clean water upon you, and you shall be clean."* —Ezekiel 36:25

The light the Holy Spirit casts upon the Word of God will produce in the believer a self-abhorrence and hatred of sin. "Then you will remember your evil ways and wicked deeds, and you will loathe yourselves for your sins and detestable practices" (Ezek. 36:31). But in God's grace, there is spiritual absolution for the penitent.

The fundamental provision of the new covenant—so vastly different from the old—is that *every sin is put away for ever*. Every sin is not only forgiven by God but also forgotten! What a contrast to the temporary, annual remission of sins that was the best the old covenant could offer.

The promised blessings could be summarized succinctly—pardon for sin, purity of heart, and most wonderful of all, the continual presence of God.

SURETY OF THE COVENANT

In the old covenant there were two parties, and its success and validity depended upon both parties faithfully discharging their undertakings. In this, Israel failed abysmally.

In the new covenant, too, there were two parties, but the difference was that Jesus assumed the obligations of surety of the covenant. A surety is one who stands good for the weaker party, and guarantees on his or her behalf that the obligations incurred under the agreement will be discharged. That is, under the terms of the agreement He undertakes to enable His weak children to keep its terms through the help of the indwelling Holy Spirit. Since He is our surety,

> *God will not justice twice demand,*
> *First at my bleeding Surety's hand,*
> *And then again at mine.*

Our part in the agreement is to cease from fleshly self-effort with a view to attaining holiness and to rely on the Holy Spirit as the agent in our sanctification. He responds to our trust by imparting both the desire and the dynamic for obedience.

The old covenant demanded *acts of obedience*. The new covenant expects an *attitude of trust* in God. This does not exclude the necessity for moral effort. We cannot lie back and leave everything to God. We will have to fight, but it will no longer be the losing battle of unaided self-effort, but "the good fight of faith" in an omnipotent God.

The glory of the new covenant—that is the expression Paul used—lies in the fact that it exactly meets the needs of failing but aspiring men and women. It was not given for only a spiritual elite, a holy club. It was designed for people who had made a mess of their lives, and therein lies its optimistic message. Let us no longer live under the forbidding shadow of the old covenant but enter into the blessings of the new covenant.

UNDER LAW TO CHRIST

It should be understood that the statement "we are not under law but under grace" does not mean that we can be artinomians—having faith but not good works—and not under any law at all. Scripture tells us that we are not under law *as a means of justification,* but we are "under Christ's law" (1 Cor. 9:21), the law of love and loyalty that makes duty and obedience a delight. We now obey God, not because we must, but because we love Him, and He has given us the impulse and the desire to obey (see Phil. 2:13).

The only way in which a better covenant could conceivably be devised would be by destroying our personality and withdrawing our free will. But this would reduce us to the status of robots, and God is not seeking robots to worship Him; He wants intelligent, responsible worshipers. As Jesus said, "A time is coming and has now come when the true worshipers will worship the Father in Spirit and in truth, for they are the kind of worshipers the Father seeks" (John 4:23).

The mature Christian will ask, "Am I in practice living under the old covenant with its imperfections, or am I living under the new covenant with its benefits and blessings?" If the answer is the former, the believer will lose no time in abandoning the old and embracing the new.

20

Unduly Premature Senility

We have much to say about this, but it is hard to explain because you are slow to learn. In fact, though by this time you ought to be teachers, you need someone to teach you the elementary truths of God's word all over again. You need milk, not solid food! Anyone who lives on milk, being still an infant, is not acquainted with the teaching about righteousness. But solid food is for the mature, *who by constant use have trained themselves to distinguish good from evil.*
—Hebrews 5:11–14, emphasis mine

Therefore let us leave the elementary teachings about Christ and go on to maturity. —Hebrews 6:1

This passage teaches that spiritual maturity is not a matter of age but of attitudes. The writer is expressing his concern at the spiritual retrogression that had taken place in the lives of the Hebrew believers to whom he wrote. If the peril of the Corinthian Christians had been that of *spiritual immaturity*—an unduly protracted infancy—the Hebrew believers were threatened with another serious peril, *spiritual retrogression*—an unduly premature spiritual senility.

Some commentators maintain that Hebrews 5:11–6:6, a notoriously difficult passage to interpret, refers to non-Christians, those whose profession of faith was only nominal. Others, as W. H. Griffith Thomas has pointed out, maintain that every prominent word in the passage is found applied to genuine believers elsewhere. If this is so, and true believers are in view, the conclusion would be that they were Christians who had once been progressing toward maturity but had regressed into a spiritual "second childhood."

The writer was bursting with eagerness to share with them the deeper truths of Christ's High Priesthood "in the order of Melchizedek" and all the attendant blessings; but he was frustrated by their spiritual insensitivity and lethargy. They had not always been like that.

SPIRITUAL SENILITY IS INDEPENDENT OF AGE

Spiritual senility is a disorder that is not confined to those who are old. It is tragic but true that, if we may coin a word, believers can *unknow* spiritual truth; they can lose their spiritual insight. Truths that once gripped and enthralled them can become a dead letter issue and leave them unmoved. The reason behind this possibility is that the apprehension of spiritual truth is not a solely intellectual exercise. It is even more a matter of illumination by the Holy Spirit, the interpreter as well as the inspirer of the Word of God. Our relation to the Holy Spirit is, therefore, of prime importance in our progress toward maturity.

"You have become dull of hearing" is the Revised Standard Version rendering of Hebrews 5:11. These believers were not always so, but for some reason deterioration had set in, and now they had become unresponsive to the voice of the Spirit. Their hearing had become less sensitive than in the early days of their first love, and they had become apathetic and listless. This attitude of mind and heart not only hinders growth but also leads to spiritual regression. There is no place for mental lassitude in the

Christian life. It is for us to "gird up the loins of our mind" and give our whole concentration to discovering what God is saying to us in His Word.

The peril of unconscious regression confronts us all. Hosea uses an appropriate figure of speech in this connection. Referring to Ephraim, he said, "His hair is sprinkled with gray, but he does not notice" (Hos. 7:9). Gray hair is usually the first sign of waning physical virility—and it has its parallel in the realm of the Spirit.

Gray hairs come painlessly and unannounced. Spiritual decline need not be conscious and deliberate. In fact, backsliding is seldom the result of willful decision. Vision and enthusiasm always tend to wane. The fire must be fueled or the flame will die. Historically the deterioration of Ephraim (here used of the whole nation of Israel), began with an unholy alliance with the ruthless and idolatrous Assyrians. This in turn led to immorality and weakened the fabric of the whole nation.

UNCONSCIOUS DETERIORATION

The warning is plain. We should be alert to detect early signs of premature spiritual senility appearing in our inner lives, for it is not too difficult to maintain spiritual appearances while inward reality is lacking.

The shock of discovery of our first gray hairs usually takes place as we stand before the mirror. Ignorance of our true condition may well be the outcome of neglecting to use the mirror of the Word, which faithfully reflects the unretouched original. Deterioration begins when we are too busy or too lazy to compare our lives with the standards of Scripture and bring them into conformity.

In Ephraim's case the tragedy lay in the words "he does not notice"—tragic and necessary ignorance. A similar tragedy, although in the physical realm, overtook

Samson, of whom it is recorded, "He did not know that the Lord had left him" (Judg. 16:20). The results in his case are a matter of history.

One way to treat gray hairs is to dye them. They may appear more youthful, but underneath they are still gray hairs. The only totally satisfactory way of dealing with them is to pull them out by the roots! Painful, but effective. Was this not what our Lord had in mind when He said, "If your right eye causes you to sin, gouge it out and throw it away"? (Matt. 5:29).

Notice the writer's three indictments of these Hebrew Christians. First, they had become sluggish in hearing God's Word and in working out the implications of discipleship (Heb. 5:11). Second, they now needed someone to re-teach them the elementary truths of the gospel (Heb. 5:12). Third, they had reverted to infancy and were unskilled in the word of righteousness (Heb. 5:13).

The Hebrew Christians now had little taste for the deeper things of the Word of God and were content with the ABCs of truth—pardon for sin, escape from hell, hope of heaven. They were still orthodox in belief, but they were sluggish in translating truth into practice. The writer feels he must arouse them by stern reproof and warning.

Spiritual immaturity in an older Christian is not an amiable weakness but a positive sin. But it is not only the older Christian who can retrogress. This can happen to younger believers who cease to acknowledge in practice the Lordship of Christ, and thus they grieve the Holy Spirit. Neglect of the culture of the inner life will exacerbate this condition.

We must be careful, however, not to despise or undervalue the elementary doctrines of the faith. While the gospel is in some senses simple, it is by no means all elementary. It begins with the simple truths but progresses toward more profound teachings, truths that baffle the profoundest philosopher.

The Hebrew Christians were exhorted to progress from the rudimentary teachings of Judaism to the final religion of Christianity. Both Paul and the author of the Book of Hebrews refer to the rudimentary teachings of Scripture as "milk"; but they do not do it in a disparaging way, for milk is neither appropriate nor sufficient for a mature adult. "Solid food is for the mature."

THREE AREAS OF REGRESSION

Let us consider three areas of deterioration that marked the condition of these believers.

Sluggishness in hearing the Word and achieving spiritual insight

The Hebrew Christians had been overcome by spiritual inertia—a condition that is still common among third-generation Christians. They were not among those who hungered and thirsted after righteousness (see Matt. 5:6). They failed to put mental and moral effort into their lives. They had forgotten that there is something we must do if we are to mature spiritually. God will not do our thinking for us, nor will He read the Bible and pray instead of us. This is our part, and if we fail to do it, our unused faculties will atrophy.

In his younger days Charles Darwin, of evolution notoriety, was an ardent devotee of both music and literature. Later, he became so engrossed in his scientific studies that music and literature were squeezed out of his daily habits.

When Darwin was about to retire from his scientific research, he looked forward with eager anticipation to once again taking up his former loves, but to his dismay he discovered that he had lost the taste for them and was quite unable to recapture his former passion for music and literature. His powers of appreciation of these art forms had atrophied through disuse. Something akin to this had overtaken the Hebrew Christians.

Their unresponsiveness to the Master's voice in His Word has a parallel in the eastern shepherd and his sheep. We are told that when a sheep does not respond to the voice of the shepherd, that is a sign that it is sick. The Good Shepherd has many sick sheep in His flock. They have lost their spiritual appetite and fall easy prey to the marauding hosts of evil who work through false teachers and false cults.

Dr. A. W. Tozer bemoaned the fact that so many Christians were not even as far advanced as they were a few years before.[1] They had known days in the past when their faith was keener, their love warmer, their tears nearer the surface, their love of prayer greater, their separation and purity brighter than now.

Thank God this condition need not be perpetuated. There is a way back!

> There is a way for man to rise
> To that sublime abode,
> An offering and a sacrifice
> A Holy Spirit's energies
> An Advocate with God.

T. Binney

Inability to teach others

> In fact, though by this time you ought to be teachers, you need someone to teach you the elementary truths of God's word all over again. —Hebrews 5:12

This is the second area of possible retrogression. The special spiritual gift of the teacher is not in view here. In its ordinary sense the art of teaching is the ability to communicate truth, and in this sense all Christians should be teachers, passing on to others the truth they have learned and experienced. This may be done in an informal as well as a formal manner. We are under obligation to share our discoveries with others who need it and can profit by it.

It is amazing the enrichment that accompanies the sharing of precious truth with another. Nothing will stimulate a jaded spiritual appetite more. The sign of maturity in Christians is that they have a zest to lead others into the satisfying experience they themselves enjoy. They delight in teaching others the progressive truths of Scripture.

> *Ceasing to give, we cease to have,*
> *Such is the law of love.*
>
> R. C. Trench

Reversion to infancy

> You need milk, not solid food! Anyone who lives on milk, being still an infant, is not acquainted with the teaching about righteousness. But solid food is for the mature. —Hebrews 5:12–14

A third evidence of spiritual degeneration is reversion to infancy. The *Corinthian* Christians were spiritual infants because of what they *did*. The *Hebrew* Christians had reverted to infancy because of what they had *failed to do*. As their appetite for the strong meat of the Word waned, their powers of digestion weakened, until they reached the stage when they could not assimilate solid food and once again had to be bottle fed.

Strong meat is for strong people, and strong meat makes strong people. A believer becomes mature through a diligent study of Scripture, which enables him or her to formulate standards of conduct that conform to the Word. The believer is careful to translate scriptural truth into practice. But these evidences were lacking in the Hebrews.

"I need to repeat to you the ABC of God's revelation to men" is J. B. Phillips' rendering of Hebrews 5:12. The affirmation "I love the simple gospel" may be good or bad. It can be good, because the gospel in its simplicity is the appropriate food for a newborn spiritual infant. The baby thrives on the iteration and reiteration of the basic gospel truth. There is a gospel for babes in Christ.

But that statement can be bad when it is on the lips of an older Christian, if it means that person has not gone on to probe the depths of the deeper truths of the gospel. The believer is confessing retrogression instead of advancement in Christian experience.

We must never undervalue "the simple gospel" in all its beauty and winsomeness, but we must progress from there until we learn to rejoice in the gospel in all its profundity. And the simple gospel is profound. It exhausted the wisdom of God. There is a gospel so simple that the little child can grasp it. That same gospel is so profound that it will tax the wisdom of the erudite philosopher. We must not allow the pious phrase to be a cloak for mental and spiritual laziness but we must give ourselves to digging the gold out of the mine of Holy Scripture.

On the other hand we should not underestimate the ability of the new Christian to assimilate some of the deeper truths. Nor should we restrict the new believer for too long to a milk diet. As one writer put it, the preacher should not complain of the immaturity of his flock if he feeds them only on milk.

Young Christians must be helped to graduate beyond:

> *Thank you Lord for saving my soul,*
> *Thank you Lord for making me whole*
> *Thank you Lord for giving to me*
> *Thy great salvation so full and free.*

While rejoicing in that ever-fresh and glorious reality, they must continue progressing toward maturity from the doctrine of justification to sanctification; from Christ's substitutionary death for us, to our identification with Him in that death. The solid food for the mature includes an understanding of what life in the heavenlies means; the authority of the believer in the warfare with Satan; the blessings attendant on Christ's High Priesthood. Such spiritual food develops muscle and sinew in the spiritual life.

THE PRESCRIPTION

Diagnosis should lead to prescription of the remedy. How can this lost ground be regained? The first step obviously is the frank confession that retrogression has taken place and that it is not only regrettable but sinful. Then complete cleansing can be claimed, and certain steps can be taken.

"Let us leave the elementary teachings about Christ" (Heb. 6:1), and move on from there. Six of these teachings are specified, all of which formed part of the teachings of Old Testament Judaism. It has been pointed out that a Hebrew Christian could abandon Christ without necessarily forsaking these doctrines. This constituted the danger of remaining in the elementary stages.

Get better acquainted with Christ who in His capacity as our High Priest secures our access to God, presents our prayers at the Father's throne, and lives to intercede for us. This is the significance of Hebrews 5:4–7. Three of His gracious activities are revealed in this epistle.

1. Christ is able to help

> *Because he himself suffered when he was tempted,*
> *he is able to help those who are being tempted.*
> —Hebrews 2:18

There are two Greek words for "help." One means "to come unsought," the other, "to come in answer to a call of need." It is a comfort to know that our High Priest knows no limitations. We are often willing to help someone in need, but we lack the ability. Our Lord is not only willing but able.

2. Christ is able to sympathize

> *For we do not have a high priest who is unable to sympathize with our weaknesses, but we have one who has been tempted in every way, just as we are—yet was without sin.* —Hebrews 4:15

Sympathy is more than mere pity. It means "to suffer together with" someone, to enter into the experience of another as though it were one's own. Sympathy is a concept entirely foreign to Greek or pagan thought. The Greek gods when they came to earth were concerned with nothing more than their own pleasure and indulgence. What a contrasting picture is the attitude of our High Priest.

3. Christ is able to save completely

> *Therefore he is able to save completely those who come to God through him, because he always lives to intercede for them.* —Hebrews 7:25

Note the present tense, indicating "a sustained experience resulting from a continuing practice"—He is able to keep on saving those who are continually coming to God.

What reassurance we can have in knowing that there is no personal problem for which He does not have a solution, no enemy from whom He cannot rescue, and no sin—whether conscious or subconscious—from which He cannot deliver.

Engage in teaching others

> *By this time you ought to be teachers.* —Hebrews 5:12

Our Lord enunciated an unchanging principle: "Whoever has will be given more" (Matt. 13:12a). The more we teach and pass on truth to others, the more truth we ourselves will understand.

We can use various tools for teaching—letters, personal conversation, telephone, radio, and TV as well as formal teaching from desk or pulpit.

Exercise your spiritual faculties.

> *Those who have their faculties trained by practice to distinguish good from evil.* —Hebrews 5:14

Spiritual gifts are developed and increased with exercise. Both Stephen and Philip began their ministry in social service, but as they were faithful in their exercise of this gift, God added others. Both men became powerful preachers of the gospel.

NOTES

1. A. W. Tozer, *I Talk Back to the Devil* (Harrisburg, Pennsylvania: Christian Publications, Inc., 1972), p. 45.

21

Satanic Hindrances to Maturity

Finally, be strong in the Lord and in his mighty power.
Put on the full armor of God so that you can take your
stand against the devil's schemes. For our struggle is
not against flesh and blood, but against the rulers,
against the authorities, against the powers of this dark
world and against the spiritual forces of evil in the
heavenly realms. Therefore put on the full armor of
God, so that when the day of evil comes, you may be
able to stand your ground, and after you have done
everything, to stand. —Ephesians 6:10–13

"A good general must penetrate the brain of his enemy." These words of Victor Hugo are equally applicable to the spiritual warfare in which the Christian is engaged. Since our adversary, Satan, is the second most powerful being in the universe, and since he is implacable in his hatred of Christ and His church, the mature Christian will want to discover the strategy and tactics of this enemy. But it is a deplorable fact that there is no area of Christian teaching in which the majority of believers are more illiterate.

Enquiry among church members reveals that ministers rarely preach about Satan. Many have confessed that they have never heard even one message about the devil and his activities. This is, of course, very gratifying to him, for his incognito is one of his winning cards. Be that as it may, it is very reprehensible on the part of leaders and preachers who have been appointed guardians of the flock. Paul could claim, "We are not unaware of his schemes" (2 Cor. 2:11), but this claim would not be true of many Christians, to their own loss.

When Lord Montgomery was appointed to command the Allied forces in the North African theater of World War II, it is instructive to learn how he set about preparing himself for that monumental task.

He did not go to North Africa to study the terrain on which the campaign was to be fought. Instead, he gave himself to the study of the background, character, training, and outlook of his opponent, Rommel. He obeyed the first rule of warfare—"Know your enemy." If he could forecast Rommel's strategy and tactics, he could take steps to forestall and foil his attacks. The mature Christian will pursue a similar course, and thus be equipped for spiritual warfare.[1]

We are in danger of running to two extremes about Satan. One is to largely ignore the devil and his works and get on with our work as if he did not exist. The other extreme is to take him too seriously and make too much of him. Believers in the Middle Ages tended to follow the latter course and gave the devil a disproportionate place in their theology and preaching. They entertained morbid fears, and as a result they lost their peace and assurance. Today, others go to the opposite extreme and do not take the devil seriously enough.

The believer must neither underestimate nor overestimate the power of Satan, nor should the believer live in fear of him. We are not to be "frightened in any way by those who oppose" us (Phil. 1:28).

But if the devil cannot make skeptics of us, he will try to make us excessively devil-conscious. He will try to make us see an evil spirit as the actor behind every sickness or adverse circumstance. Demons are blamed for sins that Scripture attributes to our own sinful natures. As James writes, "Each one is tempted when, *by his own evil desire,* he is dragged away and enticed" (James 1:14, italics mine). Instead of following Scripture and reckoning themselves dead to that sin, many people resort to the supposed exorcism of a demon by someone else.

MILITANT CHRISTIANITY

Both Jesus and Paul clearly indicated that there is a militant side to Christianity. There is the rest of faith and there is also the fight of faith. The church is involved in a fierce and truceless warfare. On His very first recorded mention of His church, our Lord spoke about it in the context of conflict with the powers of darkness:

"On this rock I will build my church, and the gates of Hades will not overcome it." —Matthew 16:18

Christ came "to destroy the works of the devil," and has appointed us to be associated with Him to that end.

The militant aspect of Christianity is not popular in some liberally slanted theological circles, and endeavors have been made to expunge this concept from both liturgy and hymnology.

In the *New Zealand Herald* of June 28, 1982, the following paragraph appeared: "The Uniting Church of Australia has launched an offensive on militaristic language. They passed a resolution to blast all references to war from their hymns and prayers. 'Onward, Christian Soliders' would have to be rewritten."

It must have been very gratifying to Satan to have the church on his side. He does not care how it is achieved, he wants to neutralize the army of the Lord.

Satan's final objective is nothing less than to eliminate God and usurp His throne. He will do anything to nullify the achievements of the Cross and to defeat, or delay as long as possible, the fulfillment of God's eternal purpose.

It appears that a credible cause of the intensification of the war, crime, and violence that abound is given in the Book of Revelation:

> Now have come the salvation and the power and the kingdom of our God, and the authority of his Christ. For the accuser of our brothers . . . has been hurled down. . . . But woe to the earth and the sea, because the devil has gone down to you! *He is filled with fury,* because he knows that his time is short. —Revelation 12:10–12, italics mine

We can expect that as the work of God prospers, as the day of the second advent draws closer, Satan's attacks will be more subtle and virulent. His fury will increase with the shortening of the time.

NAMES REVEAL CHARACTER

In His wisdom, God has chosen to reveal Himself in large measure through the names attributed to Him in the Scriptures. In an old book entitled, *The Wonderful Names of our Wonderful Lord,* T. C. Horton catalogs no fewer than 365 names and titles of God. Each of these casts some different light on facets of the divine character and work.

It is not surprising, therefore, that the same is true of the devil. There are seventeen different appellations by which he is described in Scriptures, several of which we will consider.

Satan means "adversary, opposer." This describes his activity in relation to God, Christ, and the church. Satan is antagonistic to all that is highest and best. If God is for anything, Satan is against it. He, therefore, is opposed to anything that is for the good of the church. He opposes every forward move that threatens his own kingdom.

Devil means "slanderer, traducer, accuser." In this role Satan is behind social, political, and religious agitation and revolution. Lies and smear campaigns are part of his stock-in-trade.

The devil slandered God to Adam in Eden (see Gen. 3:4–5). He slandered Job to God (see Job 1:9–11). If he can induce believers to slander or traduce one another, he has achieved a significant victory, for as the devil, his tactics are to disrupt and divide the church of God.

Beelzebub means "lord of the flies," and as such, Satan has been called the genius who presides over corruption. He corrupts and pollutes everything he touches.

He pollutes social life through drink, drugs, and debauchery. He corrupts personal life through intrigue, bribery, and insincerity. He corrupts religious life through humanism, materialism, and syncretism (or compromise).

As *"that ancient serpent"* (Rev. 12:9), Luther said of him:

> *His craft and power are great,*
> *And armed with cruel hate,*
> *On earth is not his equal.*

The wisdom with which he was endowed before his fall degenerated into evil cunning and craftiness. He works under cover, but when it suits his book, he emerges as "an angel of light." His tactics are to deceive and delude.

As *"the Great Dragon"* he appears in Revelation 12:3–8. The title was used in the past of any great monster of the land or sea. To the Greeks the dragon was a fabulous, mythical creature, ferocious and frightening. It was supposed to possess dread, malignant power—a fitting description of our adversary.

Other names and titles are Abaddon, Appolyon, murderer, liar, tempter, the evil one, roaring lion, prince and god of this world, accuser of the brethren, prince of the domain of the air.

With this light shed on Satan's character and activities, the Christian warrior need not be taken by surprise. This knowledge should help the believer penetrate the brain of the enemy; to be forewarned is to be forearmed.

STRATEGY AND TACTICS

Satan's incognito is one of his most useful weapons. It affords him comfort when prominent theologians throw doubt on his very existence. He is gratified when the world laughs at the caricatures drawn by Dante and Milton in their poetry. He is happy to be depicted with horn and hoof, for he is essentially a masquerader hiding behind differing masks suited to the occasion.

On the Cross our victorious Lord stripped away the mask and revealed the Enemy's true and diabolic nature. There "having disarmed the powers and authorities, he made a public spectacle of them, triumphing over them by the cross" (Col. 2:15).

Ruth Paxson pointed out that the devil uses two main tactics in his roles of destroyer and deceiver.

As the *destroyer* Satan wrecks civil government by inciting people to lawlessness, violence, and war. Every newspaper publishes his successes in this realm. He infiltrates society and destroys it through alcohol, drugs, and gambling. He insinuates his agents into the church, and destroys it through apostasy and the ancient heresies that are appearing as new cults. Behind all these activities is the mastermind of the devil.

As the *deceiver* Satan uses his craft and cunning to deceive "even the very elect." Augustine called him *simius dei,* the ape of God, the imitator of God.

The name is appropriate because Satan has set up his own counterfeit religious system in imitation of Christianity. He has his own *trinity*—the devil, the beast, and the false prophet (see Rev. 16:13); his own *church*—"a synagogue of Satan" (see Rev. 2:9); his own system of *theology*—"doctrines of demons" (see 1 Tim. 4:1 RSV); his own *ministers*—ministers of Satan (see 2 Cor. 11:14–15); his own *sacrificial system*—"the sacrifices of pagans are offered to demons" (see 1 Cor. 10:20); his own *communion service*—"the cup of demons . . . and the table of demons" (see 1 Cor. 10:21); his own *gospel*—"a different gospel—which is really no gospel at all" (see Gal. 1:6b–7a); his own *throne* and his own *worshipers* (see Rev. 13:2, 4).

Satan has thus developed a thorough religious system that is an imitation of Christianity. In his role as the imitator of God, he inspires *false christs*, self-constituted messiahs (see Matt. 24:4–5). He uses *false teachers* who specialize in his "theology," and bring in "destructive heresies, even denying the sovereign Lord who bought them" (2 Pet. 2:1). These teachers are adept at mixing truth and error in such proportions as to make error palatable.

The devil sends out *false prophets,* in keeping with the Lord's prophecy, "and many false prophets will appear and deceive many people" (Matt. 24:11). He introduces *false brethren* into the church. "Some false brothers had infiltrated our ranks to spy on the freedom we have in Christ Jesus and to make us slaves" (Gal. 2:4). He sponsors *false apostles* who imitate the true. "Such men are false apostles . . . masquerading as apostles of Christ" (2 Cor. 11:13).

THE DEFEATABILITY OF SATAN

A firm belief in the defeatability of Satan is one of the strongest weapons in the Christian's arsenal. For us to highlight Satan's power without taking into account Christ's victory over him at Calvary is like talking about the Napoleonic wars without mentioning the decisive battle of Waterloo.

Although Satan is the second most powerful being in the universe, *he is not omnipotent*. He possesses no power at all independent of God. He has a wonderfully effective communications system through his demons, but *he is not omnipresent*. He possesses great subtlety and shrewdness, but *he is not omniscient*. He has to gather his information as we do. He is no match for our omnipotent, omniscient, and omnipresent Lord.

James 4:7 has been termed the most incredible verse in the Bible: "Submit yourselves, then, to God. *Resist the devil and he will flee from you*" (italics mine). It does seem incredible that this powerful, malignant being who controls hell's legions, who could offer the kingdoms of the world to Christ, will flee before the weakest believer who resists him on the grounds of the victory of the Cross. But it is gloriously true! We can go into every moral and spiritual battle with the assurance in advance of complete victory.

So we may say that Satan's power, though great, is not inherent, but delegated. It is not unlimited, but controlled (see Job 1:12; 2:6). It is not invincible, but shattered (see Luke 11:21–22). It is not triumphant, but doomed (see Rev. 20:10). The believer can shout in triumph:

> *Jesus is stronger than Satan and sin,*
> *Satan to Jesus must bow.*
> *Therefore I triumph without and within,*
> *Jesus saves me now!*

> A.C.D.

It is also true that any expectation Christians have of being overcomers in the warfare with Satan must lie outside themselves. Believers have no inherent spiritual resources to draw upon to enable them to meet and defeat their wily and experienced enemy.

With force of arms we nothing can,
Full soon were we down-ridden;
But for us fights the proper Man,
Whom God Himself hath bidden.
Ask ye who is this same?
Christ Jesus is His name,
The Lord Sabaoth's Son,
He and no other one
Shall conquer in the battle.

Martin Luther

The believer's only hope is to lay hold of the victory Christ gained over Satan, first in the desert and finally on the Cross (see 1 John 3:8; Col. 2:15; Luke 11:18–19). These and many other verses attest to the stunning defeat Satan suffered at the Cross.

Since Calvary, "the accuser of the brethren" (Rev. 12:10) has no power or right to charge the believer with sin before the throne of God. Since then the vaunted power of the usurper is only an empty show. We remain under his power either because we do not know or do not exercise the authority over this vanquished foe that has been delegated to us by God.

I hear the Accuser roar
Of evils I have done,
I know them all and thousands more,
Jehovah findeth none.

Isaac Watts

NOTES

1. J. Oswald Sanders, *Satan Is No Myth* (Chicago: Moody Press, 1975), p. 71.

22

The Dynamic
for Maturity

*Never be lacking in zeal, but keep your spiritual fervor,
serving the Lord.* —Romans 12:11

*Never let your zeal flag, maintain the holy glow, serve
the Lord.* —Romans 12:11 MOFFATT

With unflagging zeal, in ardor of spirit, serve the Lord.
—Romans 12:11 NEB

Each of the above renderings conveys the idea of the
glowing zeal and fervor that should characterize the mature
Christian. In his translation of the verse, Archbishop
Harrington C. Lees introduced the thought that in the
central clause it is the Holy Spirit who is referred to rather
than the human spirit. His rendering is, "kept at boiling
point by the Holy Spirit, doing bondservice for the
Master." The suggestion is appropriate, for the verb used
means, "to bubble or boil." Only the indwelling and
inworking Holy Spirit can enable our zeal to be maintained
and our spirits to glow.

A threefold activity is in view in this verse. First, the
believer must be diligent. If we are to attain maturity there
is no room for laziness or foot-dragging. The enduement of
the Spirit is the source of zeal and diligence in the work of
the kingdom. Second, a central furnace glows in the depths
of the human spirit to maintain that zeal at boiling-point in

spite of all the surrounding cooling influences of an inhospitable world. Third, the believer is a willing slave, doing "bondservice for the Master."

While the Christian is privileged to enjoy "the rest of faith," this does not necessarily mean rest of body. Follow the journeyings of the apostle Paul, and you will be astounded at the intense activity his zeal involved him in. There was no slackness or slothfulness in his service. Luther's rendering of Romans 12:11 highlights this aspect: "In regard to zeal be not lazy." He knew that zeal and laziness could never run in double harness. Only when we have done well will the Lord say, "Well done!"

When, with uplifted whip, Jesus drove the rapacious traders and mercenary priests and money-changers out of the temple, the disciples were astounded at the change in the Master. Never before had they seen in Him such burning indignation. The occasion of His anger was the desecration of His Father's house, which was intended as a house of prayer for all nations. The priests and traders had converted it into a thieves' kitchen.

"Get these things out of here!" Christ thundered. "How dare you turn my Father's house into a market!" (see Mark 11:17).

The disciples were at a loss to explain this flaming anger, until they remembered an Old Testament prophecy: "His disciples remembered that it is written: 'Zeal for your house will consume me'" (John 2:17). With His example before us, we are exhorted, "Never let your zeal flag; maintain the holy glow."

The last clause "serve the Lord," suggests the motivation: "Doing bondservice for the Master." These words are pictorial and are drawn from Exodus 21:2–6.

When an Israelite was sold into slavery for debt or some other cause, his master could compel him to serve for only six years. Then he must set the slave free. If, however, the slave considered that the benefits of serving a kind master outweighed the sweets of liberty, he could elect to stay in his master's service. In that event a ceremony was held, and his ear was bored as a permanent seal on the transaction—a sign that he had chosen to remain a servant for life.

His was now a different kind of servitude. He was bound and yet free because he now served his master out of love, not out of duty or compulsion. The words he spoke at the ceremony gave the reason for his choice: "I love my master . . . and do not want to go out free." It is in the same spirit that the mature Christian serves his or her Lord.

THE CENTRAL FURNACE

The middle clause of the text suggests the central furnace: "kept at boiling point by the Holy Spirit." It is not too difficult to come to "boiling point" in Christian experience when the Lord draws especially near, or when one is at a gathering where the Spirit is manifestly working in power; but it is quite another thing to stay there. It is with the soul as with the body—the tendency is always to give off heat, not to generate greater heat. Only through the Holy Spirit's work can this tendency be reversed.

When my son was a boy, we visited one of the boiling lakes in the thermal regions of New Zealand. The guide told the boy to throw a shovelful of sand into the steaming lake. When he did so, immediately the water began to bubble and boil and showed no signs of abating. On being asked for an explanation of the phenomenon, the guide said it was very simple.

The water in the lake was very acid, and the sand was iron sand. What we were observing was simply the result of the chemical action of the acid on the iron sand deep down in the lake. He said the disturbance would continue for twenty-four hours, until all the iron had been consumed.

In this incident I saw an illustration of the secret of the Lord's fervent zeal. The Holy Spirit, working in the depths of His spirit, ungrieved by sin, enabled Him to maintain the holy glow and remain constantly at boiling point. As the acid consumed the iron, so zeal for God's glory consumed His Son.

In his immortal allegory, *The Pilgrim's Progress,* John Bunyan depicts Christian paying a visit to Interpreter's house. As Christian approached, he saw a fire burning on the hearth and a man pouring water on it. He was mystified to observe that instead of quenching the flames, they seemed only to leap higher. But when he went around to the back of the fire, he discovered the explanation. There he saw another man pouring oil on the fire!

Bunyan's illustration finds its counterpart in Christian experience. In our straining toward spiritual maturity, there are many people, influences, and circumstances that would quench and try to extinguish our zeal and enthusiasm for God and His work. In the unceasing activity of the Holy Spirit in our hearts, we have the divine panacea.

The Holy Spirit constantly pours on the oil that more than counteracts the effects of the water. Indeed, He turns the water into steam that generates new power to maintain a life aglow for God. It is He who motivates and sustains our service for the Master.

UNLIMITED RESOURCES

Few exploit to the full the unlimited resources that are available to the Christian in the ministry of the Holy Spirit. Christ presents us with what might be termed a carte blanche to the rich spiritual blessings that are ours in Him. "If you then though you are evil, know how to give good gifts to your children, *how much more* will your Father in heaven give the Holy Spirit to those who ask him!''(Luke 11:13, italics mine). These blessings become ours in experience only through the appropriation of faith.

At first sight the passage presents a very real problem. It is the teaching of Scripture that every genuine believer has the Holy Spirit dwelling within. This is made clear in Romans 8:9, ''If anyone does not have the Spirit of Christ, he does not belong to Christ.'' This verse leaves us in no doubt.

But if every Christian already has the Spirit, what would be the point in asking for what one already has? Viewed from this angle, Luke 11:13 seems to be redundant. And yet one does not expect the words of Christ to be redundant.

There is a satisfying explanation that uncovers a rich vein of truth. In the English New Testament, the phrase ''the Holy Spirit'' occurs eighty-eight times, and always with the definite article. In the Greek New Testament, however, the definite article occurs in only fifty-four cases, while in thirty-four instances it is just ''Holy Spirit,'' with no definite article. Luke 11:13 is one of the latter instances. What is the significance of the different usage?

Dr. H. B. Swete has pointed out that in the Greek, where the definite article is used—''the Holy Spirit''—the reference is to the Holy Spirit as a person. But where there is no definite article—just ''Holy Spirit''—the reference is not to Him as a person, but to His operations and manifestations.

When on the Day of Pentecost the disciples are spoken of as being ''filled with the Spirit,'' the definite article is omitted. The reference there is to the operations of the Holy Spirit that accompanied and followed the gift of the Holy Spirit as an indwelling person.

Here is a most exhilarating and encouraging truth, which opens up great possibilities to the believer. What the passage seems to mean can be expressed this way: "If you then who are evil know how to give good gifts to your children, how much more will your heavenly Father give [that operation of] the Holy Spirit [that is needed to enable a godly life and an effective ministry] to those who ask Him." The verse, far from being redundant, conveys an open promise that just awaits our appropriation.

What then is the operation of the Spirit that is needed to produce spiritual maturity and equip for effective service? *"How much more* will your heavenly Father" impart that operation when you ask for it?

Is it *love* that is lacking? Ask the Father for it. Romans 5:5 assures us that "God has poured out this love into our hearts by the Holy Spirit, whom he has given to us." Claim it!

Is it *joy?* Joy in the Holy Spirit is available. Claim it!

Is it *power* for effective service? The Master promised, "You will receive power when the Holy Spirit comes on you" (Acts 1:8). Ask for it and claim it!

Is *personal purity* the problem? As the Spirit of holiness, He imparts purity. Ask the Father for it and believe that He keeps His Word!

Is it *utterance* to present the truth effectively? At Pentecost the disciples spoke "as the Spirit gave them utterance" (Acts 2:4 KJV). Ask for it and claim it!

Is it *wisdom* in making decisions and solving problems? As the Spirit of wisdom (see Isa. 11:2), He will fulfill the promise, "If any of you lacks wisdom, he should ask God, who gives generously to all without finding fault, and it will be given to him" (James 1:5). Ask for it and claim it!

Is it *patience?* Since the fruit of the Spirit is patience (see Gal. 5:22), ask for it and claim it!

These are only a few of the operations of the Spirit that come within the scope of this wonderful verse. The reader can compile his or her own list. Let us give full weight to the Lord's words of assurance—*"how much more!''* Our heavenly Father will act even more generously than the kindest earthly Father. Why do we not trust Him more implicitly and daringly?

It should be noted that these operations of the Spirit are promised only "to those who ask him." We can and do fail to experience them for reasons that James gives: "You do not have, because you do not ask God" (James 4:2). There is no question about the Father's willingness to impart. The problem lies in our failing to receive. God cannot be both giver and receiver.

James suggests another reason why this promise may be of small benefit to us. The believer may ask for some operation of the Spirit, "but when he asks, he must believe and not doubt . . . He who doubts . . . should not think he will receive anything from the Lord" (James 1:6–7).

So the dynamic for maturity is the Holy Spirit Himself, working unhindered in the believer who has committed his or her life to the Spirit's control.

If our faith were but more simple,
We would take Him at His word,
And our lives would be all sunshine
In the sweetness of the Lord.
                    F. W. Faber

Index to Scripture References

14:50 169
16:17 82

Luke
8:46 43
10:17 81
10:19 81
11:9–10 79
11:13 211
11:18–19 205
11:21–22 204
14:25–35 60
14:26 64
14:27 64
14:33 64
14:28–30 63
22:27 42
24:27 62
24:45 168

John
2:17 208
3:31–32 61
4:23 184
4:36 44
6:60, 66 61
6:66 63
7:17 171
8:31 .... 59, 68
12:24 54
13:5 59
13:15–16 43
13:34–35 65
14:15–18 168
14:17 168
15:7 67
15:8 59
15:11 41
15:16 43
15:26 170
16:14 170
16:23 86
17:4 40
18:36 88

20:19 169
20:29 50

Acts
1:8 212
2:4 212
2:14–16 182
2:46–47 169
10:38 166
16:25 54
24:16 143

Romans
1:13 44
2:14–15 143
5:3 134
5:5 .... 46, 212
6:6, 11, 14 52
6:14 52
6:19 ..... 151, 160
7:21–24 178
8:1 149
8:3 178
8:8 178
8:9 211
8:13 141
8:26, 27 ... 79, 80, 170
8:29 173
8:35–37 102
10:17 52
12:1–2 159
12:2 .... 44, 71
12:3 162
12:6–8 ... 163, 165
12:9–10 166
12:11 207
15:13 52

1 Corinthians
1:7 .... 21, 28
3:1 28
3:1–2 27
3:1–3 21

3:3 33
3:4 33
3:13 92
8:7 ...... 146, 147
9:21 184
9:25 ... 87, 139–40
9:26–27 140
10:6, 11 29
10:12 95
10:13 91
10:20–21 203
11:1 21
12:3 171
12:11 20
13:1–3 67
14:32 164
15:9 160
16:15 164

2 Corinthians
2:11 198
2:14–16 . 119, 120, 121, 123
3:3 179
3:7–8 177
3:17–18 167
3:18 ... 9, 24, 163, 169, 172
4:16 72
5:7 50
5:11 127
10:4 81
10:4–5 139
10:12 38
11:13 203
11:14–15 203
11:23–29 . 101–102
12:7–10 105
12:9 .... 45, 132
12:10 .... 103, 132

Galatians
1:7 203
2:4 203

Index to Persons